Dyslexia

An Explanation

An explanation for the signs and symptoms of dyslexia

Martin F. Murphy

FLYLEAF PRESS

First published in 2004

Flyleaf Press
4 Spencer Villas
Glenageary, Co. Dublin
Ireland
e-mail: flyleaf@indigo.ie
www.flyleaf.ie

British Library cataloguing in Publication Data available

ISBN 0 9539974-5-6

The information in this book is subject to change without notice.

Design: Shay Kennedy – *MacArt*
Typesetting: Harry McCue – *McCue Typesetting*

Dedicated to all parents, who sometimes struggle to understand their children and especially to my own mother

my mother, my confidence.

Acknowledgments

My family and friends who have been both patient and tolerant in the extreme for putting up with my near obsessive conversations about dyslexia over this last number of years.

I wish to recognise the Staff and Board of Management of Clonkeen College Dublin who were a source of motivation. Teachers who have successfully applied mental strategies originating from the dyslexia@bay™ model to help students with dyslexia, especially: Avril Watson (Burrow National School Dublin) Aine Murphy (Harold School Co. Dublin) Maire McGrath (St. Bride's Primary School Belfast) and Sam Robinson (Ashfield Girls' School Belfast).

Orla Callan-Terry and Lesley Milton who helped collate and categorise the question and answer format layout within the book in a logical sequence and whose critical comments were especially valuable. I also thank them for their enthusiasm, common sense and endless patience.

Contents

Chapter I

Dyslexia

An explanation

Introduction

I have addressed a large number of audiences in the last few years on the topic of dyslexia: The National Parents' Council (NPC), The National Association Principals and Deputy Principals (NAPD), Public Libraries, The Irish Learning Support Association (ILSA), Youthreach Programmes. I have conducted workshops for Teachers' Centres, for Parents' Associations and for teachers from over one hundred schools in Ireland, at both primary and secondary level. These audiences included parents, teachers, school principals, educational psychologists, adults with dyslexia and others working with people who have dyslexia. I have noticed that the same questions recur time and time again. This book is written as a direct response to those questions to aid an understanding of how individuals with dyslexia process information.

After teaching in the classroom for over twenty years, I have found that all the children I have taught have had different ways of learning! I repeat all children, and that includes all children with dyslexia. Having worked extensively with people who have been labelled as having dyslexia, over a long period of time, I can categorically say that no two people, children or adults, labelled as having dyslexia, have been the same.

The purpose of this book is to encourage both those working in education, and parents, to appreciate that all children, and indeed adults, with dyslexia learn differently and to gain some understanding of the specific ways in which they learn differently. Hence, the emphasis throughout the book is on the importance of finding out in detail how each person with dyslexia thinks so that a personal programme can be designed and tailored to the needs of the individual concerned to get the best possible result.

My aim is to explain the symptoms and thinking processes of those who have dyslexia. The language in the book is "non jargon" and everyday terminology is used, as far as possible, so that parents, teachers and others involved in education can understand more deeply those who have dyslexia.

Learning differences and learning difficulties

Each of us has learning differences and in some cases these learning differences are also learning difficulties.

If someone is unable to learn to play golf with a scratch handicap i.e. 0, it can be said that they have a learning difficulty playing golf because they cannot learn to play as well as a professional golfer. Similarly, if someone is unable to learn to play tennis well enough to become a Wimbledon champion, it can be said that they have a learning difficulty playing tennis (albeit a very slight one if they are runner-up in a Wimbledon final!). Some people are able to learn to speak foreign languages easily and fluently. Other people have a learning difficulty with languages and may have learned a foreign language at school over several years yet not describe themselves as fluent. Some people have difficulty learning to drive a car, some people have difficulty learning how to cook a meal, some people have difficulty learning how to play bridge etc.

However, it should also be noted that learning differences can also lead to exceptional talents – Tiger Woods appears to have learned to play golf rather differently!!

When a child is at school, learning differences that are also learning difficulties take on a new significance. It usually means having difficulties with reading, writing and spelling and such difficulties are given the name dyslexia.

Every single person with dyslexia that I have encountered has been different. Some are wonderful at art, whilst others have been very clumsy with a pen or pencil. Some are exceptionally gifted at mathematics, whilst others have had difficulty learning tables. Some are exceptional at various sports, whereas others have been very clumsy. Some are brilliant at reading and writing music, whereas others have been tone deaf. Some are wonderful with mechanical devices whereas others have appeared to be inept. The list is almost never ending.

We are all aware of famous individuals who have or had dyslexia, such as Albert Einstein, Thomas Edison, Winston Churchill, Susan Hampshire, Richard Branson and Steven Redgrave *(See Chapter 19 for more)*. These are, or have been, exceptionally talented people but in many different fields!

Characteristics of individuals with dyslexia

In Chapter 3 you will find a detailed list of the signs and symptoms of dyslexia. No person with dyslexia would have all of these; some may have only a few, whilst others may exhibit a larger number. Dyslexia is not a well-defined example of cause and effect. There are many, many different causes and the effects of those causes are unique for each individual.

If we bring a car to a garage because it has a puncture we expect the mechanic to remove the wheel and fix the puncture. However, if we bring a car to the garage because it is overheating we do not expect the mechanic to remove the wheel. It is important that the solution to a problem addresses the cause of a problem.

If each individual person with dyslexia has different problems and different gifts then the solution to the problems has to have a different emphasis for each individual.

When people are screened for dyslexia, by an Educational Psychologist they are asked to identify certain words, spell certain words, read a passage from a book, identify certain sounds, put together certain shapes and demonstrate various other skills. The person is observed during all of this and the degree of accuracy and the time taken for each task is measured. These measurements are then compared to those of others of the same age and background, and thus the degree of the "learning difficulty" is

3

established. Using these measurements the Educational Psychologist can establish whether an individual has dyslexia or not and, if so, to what degree (Chapter 18).

A unique structured approach for each person who has dyslexia

Over the years I have observed many different traits of many different people with dyslexia. I became particularly interested in the differences between the thought processes of individuals exhibiting the indications of dyslexia and the thought processes of average students who do not have difficulty with reading, writing and spelling. In addition, I became interested in the link between particular thought processes and the particular areas of the brain involved. I experimented over many years and studied many other people's work. It is as a result of these investigations that the dyslexia@bay™ System has evolved.

This book has been written for two purposes. Firstly, it is to encourage parents and teachers to appreciate that all children are different and that all children have learning difficulties of one sort or another, which are different for each individual child. By reading this book and carrying out the demonstrations it is hoped that the reader will gain an insight into how people think differently and, as a result, learn differently. By appreciating the differences in thinking styles, learning styles and types of difficulty, the reader will have a greater understanding of the child concerned and the type of help required.

Secondly the purpose of this book is to give parents, teachers and those involved in the field of dyslexia an insight into (a) how to understand, and relate, to the unique learning profile of each child with dyslexia and (b) what is necessary to design a learning programme suitable for the individual needs of each child. If each individual child with dyslexia is different then the solutions to their difficulties should be individually tailored.

It should be noted at this point, that many of the references made throughout this book allude to children with dyslexia. The approach is also designed to assist adults with dyslexia; in fact, the oldest adult to benefit from this approach was 82 years of age.

The principles of the dyslexia@bay™ System

1. Every person with dyslexia is an individual exhibiting different indications of dyslexia and hence different learning difficulties.

2. The underlying causes of an individual's symptoms have to be identified before the individual's symptoms and consequential learning difficulties can be alleviated. It is essential to understand how an individual with dyslexia thinks in order to be able to design a suitable programme of help to enable him to cope better in his normal environment. In the case of a child the focus is enabling that child to cope better in a normal school environment.

3. Parents are wonderful teachers - they have taught their children to listen, talk, walk, run, play games, socialise with adults, socialise with their peers etc. before they first attend school. The parents of children with dyslexia are generally totally committed to their children and are a wonderful resource that the dyslexia@bay™ System recognises and utilises.

Many of the indications of dyslexia are discussed in this book together with the thought processes, which give rise to them. The book is written in a question and answer format and, whilst each question and answer can be considered in isolation, it is best to work through the book from beginning to end. Some of the later chapters such as Chapter 11 which explains in basic terms how the eyes see and Chapter 16 which describes the dyslexia@bay™ model of the brain are more detailed and are not essential to a basic understanding of the thought processes which give rise to dyslexia.

As well as a question and answer format the book includes numerous "demonstrations". Please follow the instructions of these demonstrations, as they will give you an insight into how different people think and in particular how people with dyslexia think.

Once we experience for ourselves how children with dyslexia think, not only will we sympathise more with the difficulties these children face on a daily basis but we will also have a much greater understanding of the causes of these difficulties. The greater the degree of understanding, the greater will be the motivation to implement the dyslexia@bay^{TM} System.

If, after reading the book, you wish to know more about the dyslexia@bay™ System please visit our web site:

www.dyslexia-at-bay.com

Chapter 2

How exactly do we all learn differently?

We all learn by using our senses, mainly our senses of sight, hearing and touch - we see things, we hear things and we do things. However, people often have a preference for one or other of the senses when they learn. In this book we refer to people who learn best by seeing things as visual learners, people who learn best by hearing things as auditory learners, and people who learn best by doing things as practical/kinaesthetic learners.

How do visual learners prefer to learn?

Visual learners will learn best in the classroom environment by looking at the black/white board, by seeing diagrams and words on an overhead projector and by looking at written words, pictures and diagrams in books. When visual learners understand something they will use phrases like: " I can see it now", "I have the big picture now", "I can see how it all fits together", "It is much clearer to me now". The language they use reflects the fact that they prefer to use their sense of sight when they learn.

When reading a book visual learners will first of all say the words to themselves and then make a picture in their head of what they have read. They will visualise the different characters in the book and know exactly what each one looks like in their mind. The pictures they make may be either still pictures similar to a photograph or moving pictures similar to a video or film. Visual learners will very often say that they can remember something because they can "see" where it is in the book.

When revising for exams visual learners will lay out their notes in a visually structured manner and may underline with various colours or use coloured markers so that certain names or phrases stand out. Visual learners may draw diagrams to summarise their work e.g. spider diagrams.

How do auditory learners prefer to learn?

Auditory learners will learn best in the classroom environment by listening to what the teacher says and will enjoy class discussions. To learn something, auditory learners will very often say something to themselves over and over again so that they will remember it. When auditory learners understand something they will use phrases like: "I understand what you are saying now", "It all sounds as if it makes sense now", "I can hear the full story now".

When auditory learners read a book they will see the words and say the words to themselves inside their head. They will appreciate the language used and will enjoy the flow of words. They will enjoy the different tones of voice and accents used by different characters in the book.

When revising for exams auditory learners may well read their notes out loud to themselves. When they read through their notes they will occasionally stop to repeat an important point to themselves. Auditory learners like to study in a room that is quiet and without any noise, which would be sensed as a distraction. Some auditory learners may like to record their notes onto an audiotape and play it back to themselves.

How do practical/kinaesthetic learners prefer to learn?

Practical/kinaesthetic learners will learn best in the classroom environment by doing things. At a young age they will like to learn the letters by making them out of modelling clay, will enjoy drawing with paint and feeling the paintbrush on the paper. Young practical/kinaesthetic learners will like to "act out a part" so that they can appreciate what a character in a book feels like. When practical/kinaesthetic learners understand something they will use phrases like: "I'm getting a feel for that now", "I have a handle on that now", "I am getting in touch with this subject now", "I am more comfortable with that idea now".

When practical/kinaesthetic learners read a book they read the words and try to get a feel for the action and the emotions felt by the characters. The sounds of the characters' voices and the visual imagery of the characters are not paramount for the practical/kinaesthetic learner.

When revising for exams practical/kinaesthetic learners may like to write out their notes several times just to get the "feel" of them. Some practical/kinaesthetic learners like to play with a pencil in their hands when they are studying. They will want the room that they study in to be "comfortable". They may prefer to wear loose clothing.

How do you prefer to learn?
Demonstration:

The following three short passages are written in the three different sensory styles. Read them and find which appeals to you most.

Visual style

The young girl walked through the forest. She could see the bright sunlight coming through the dark green summer foliage and falling on the brown beech leaves left from last autumn. She could see the bright green spring moss growing on the side of the aged tree trunks. She looked and could see the glint of light on the stream and the white foam nestling behind the grey green stones. She continued along the winding path until she caught sight of her grandmother's cottage with its yellow straw thatched roof and white painted walls. As she approached the dark green door with its brass knob she pushed opened the door and walked across the black and red quarry tiled floor. She saw the gleaming copper pot upon the stove and removed the lid see what was inside.

Auditory style

The young girl walked through the forest humming her favourite tune to herself. As she listened to the wind rustling through the leaves of the tall trees above her head she could hear the crack of dead twigs under foot. She

9

could also hear the crunch of last year's autumn leaves beneath her feet. The babble of the water to her left seemed to converse with the idle chatter in her head. She came upon her grandmother's cottage and lifted the brass doorknocker and let it fall with a harsh metallic thud. There was no welcoming voice from inside. She opened the door with a creak and walked across the tiled floor listening to the click of the heels of her new shoes. She could hear the pot bubbling merrily away on the stove. She put her hand on the handle of the lid asking herself what would she find in the pot.

Practical/kinaesthetic style

The young girl walked through the forest and she could feel the twigs breaking underneath her feet and the crunch of the dead leaves that fell from the trees last autumn. She ran her fingers over the rough, moss covered bark of a large tree that leaned precariously over the path that she walked along. She stopped for a moment and let the water from the stream run through her fingers. She then brushed her forehead with her hand and felt cool refreshing water against her forehead. She could sense the shiny smooth stones of the riverbank underneath her feet. When she came to the cottage she grasped the heavy brass doorknocker and felt the thud as it announced her presence. There was no answer so she pushed the door and it yielded to her weight. She walked across the smooth quarry tiled floor and put her hand on handle of the copper pot and felt the vibration of the bubbling soup inside.

Having read through the three previous passages you will find that one appeals to you more than the others; this will indicate which learning style you prefer.

How do learning differences arise and what are the implications?

Athletes build up different muscles depending upon which sport they play. A person trained to lift heavy weights will have a different body shape from a person who runs a long-distance race. By training for different events we change the shape of our body and more specifically increase the power and efficiency of different muscle groups within our body. This is well known but what is not quite so well known is that we can also train our brains and even train specific parts of our brains so that those parts perform with more power and efficiency.

Different parts of our brain are responsible for visual thoughts, auditory thoughts and practical/kinaesthetic thoughts. If our preference is for visual learning the part of our brain responsible for visual thoughts will be exercised regularly and will therefore become more powerful and efficient. If our preference is for auditory learning the part of our brain responsible for auditory thoughts will be exercised regularly and will therefore become more powerful and efficient and similarly for practical/kinaesthetic learners. As each of us develops one part of the brain more than another, we actually train the brain to function differently, consequently, we all learn differently!

No-one is exclusively visual, auditory or practical/kinaesthetic - we are a cocktail of all three. The proportion of each characteristic varies from individual to individual. As a result no two people learn in exactly the same way and the corollary of this is that no two people who have a learning difficulty "not learn" in the same way.

If we are to successfully help people who have learning difficulties we must appreciate that they are all individuals and that there are many and various reasons why they are finding learning difficult! We must look not only at the symptoms but also at the underlying reasons why people have these symptoms.

The dyslexia@bay™ System identifies these reasons and establishes a person's individual learning profile. Once a learning profile has been identified then we can successfully help the student to overcome his learning difficulties.

Chapter 3

What are the signs and symptoms of dyslexia?

I have listed below some of the signs and symptoms of dyslexia. Please remember that each individual with dyslexia will have some of these symptoms, but not all. Some students who do not have dyslexia will also exhibit some of these signs and symptoms and it is only if the student exhibits a number of these symptoms after two years at primary school that any course of action should be taken. A reasonable benchmark would be that if a student exhibited five or more of these symptoms then it may be appropriate for the student to be screened for dyslexia. If a screening test suggests that the student may have dyslexia then, and only then, should the student be referred to an Educational Psychologist for a full psychological assessment.

It should also be noted that if one attended a lecture on a new disease called Yebowa-Yebowa and the lecturer outlined a series of three symptoms such as a slight ringing in the ears, a slight sweating of the palms of the hands and an itchiness on the tip of the nose then a significant percentage of the audience would in fact actually become aware of those symptoms. This is the power of suggestion and, by raising the audience's awareness of the nose, eyes and palms; the members of the audience would seek a sensation. It has been my experience that, if a parent reads this list and then checks the child for some of the symptoms, they may get a false result. However, if when reading through this list of symptoms with the child, you and the child can identify some of them together, the results are likely to be useful and significant.

The signs and symptoms of dyslexia are listed under four headings: -

Difficulties associated with reading

Difficulties associated with writing

Difficulties associated with spelling

Non-language difficulties associated with dyslexia

Difficulties associated with reading

Hesitant and laboured reading, especially when reading loud.

Using finger to run underneath the line while reading.

Reading the same line again/skipping lines when reading.

Reading half way along a line and then continuing to read the line below.

Reading some words backwards e.g. "was" for "saw", "on" for no.

Making anagrams of words e.g. "tired" for "tried", "wives" for "views".

Leaving out words/inserting words that are not there.

Mixing up words that start with the same letters e.g. there, that, those, then, the.

Difficulty remembering/understanding what has been read.

Difficulty extracting the most important points from a passage.

Ignoring punctuation, e.g. not pausing for commas etc.

Difficulties associated with writing

Poor standard of written work compared to oral ability.

Layout of written work of a poor standard.

Losing the point of the story being written.

Lack of punctuation, or totally inappropriate use of punctuation.

Letters, syllables and words omitted, inserted or in the wrong order.

Writing letters the wrong way round. (Mirror writing)

Spelling the same word several different ways in the same passage.

Difficulty starting to write each line at the margin.

Difficulty writing along the ruled line of the page.

Difficulties associated with spelling

Wrong choice of letters due to poor auditory discrimination.

Reverse confusion with letters that look alike e.g. b/d, p/q.

Inverse confusion writing n as u, m as w.

Confusion between similar sounding words e.g. "one" and "won".

Writing letters in the wrong order e.g. time is spelt tmie.

Omitting letters in words e.g. lip for limp.

Adding inappropriate letters e.g. whent for went.

Inability to write down a word even when the letters are dictated.

Inability to identify the appropriate letter when given a sound.

Non-language difficulties associated with dyslexia

Often accused of not listening or paying attention.

Difficulty following a set of instructions.

Often accused of been unable to concentrate.

Difficulty clapping to a simple rhythm or dancing "in time".

Difficulty tying shoelaces or a tie.

Poor sense of direction and/or confusion between left and right.

Difficulty remembering the days of the week, months of the year etc.

Some symptoms of dyspraxia.

Poor sense of time awareness

Lacking in self-confidence, having a poor self-image and low self-esteem.

In conclusion, it is important to appreciate that there is a wide variety of signs and symptoms and that some of the indications are seemingly contradictory. For example, a student with dyslexia may also be somewhat clumsy but, at the other end of the scale, another student with dyslexia may be excellent at sport and games and very well coordinated.

Please note that, as a general rule, five or more of the above signs and symptoms may indicate that an individual has dyslexia.

Chapter 4

How do most students learn to spell?

Before we look at how we learn to spell, let us consider briefly how we use our memory to remember spellings. In Chapter 2 we discussed how we all learn differently – some of us are visual learners, some of us are auditory learners and some of us are practical/kinaesthetic learners.

What are the different types of memory?

There are three different types of memory corresponding to these three sensory styles – visual memory, auditory memory and practical/kinaesthetic memory.

Visual memory:

Is used to remember a picture in our mind e.g. a place we have been, a face that we know or a house that we have visited.

Auditory memory:

Is used to remember sounds e.g. the words of a song, a poem or a nursery rhyme.

Kinaesthetic (practical) memory:

Is used when we remember how to do something with our body, e.g. swinging a golf club or a tennis racket, kicking a football or casting a fishing rod.

As you will see below most children first learn to spell in school by sound (i.e. phonetically), that is to say by using their auditory memory, and then progress naturally to spelling by sight using their visual memory.

How are most students taught to spell in school?

At school most students are first taught to recognise letters and their associated sounds. They then progress to recognising short words and the sounds associated with those words. This phonetic strategy, using the sounds of words, seems to suit most students and by introducing words with similar sounds they learn to generalise spellings.

For example: bad

Dad

had

lad

mad

sad

By using this method students learn to spell several words just by changing one or two letters of a known word. In the above example, the student learns to spell and identify six words by learning to spell one particular sound, in this case the "ad" sound. The student is then introduced to short sentences, which contain the words that have been learned individually. For most students, this method is very useful for about half of the words in the English language that are spelt phonetically i.e. as they sound. It is not a coincidence that the list of the 100 words most often miss-spelt by children contain words that are not spelt as they sound e.g. their, through, clothes, people, believe, because, thought. *(see appendix)*

This phonetic method works very well in shallow orthographic languages, e.g. Italian and Spanish in which most of the words are spelt as they sound. However, English is a deep orthographic language, less than half the words being spelt as they sound. Consequently, the phonetic method of spelling is less useful.

Teaching students to spell words by sound has the advantage that it gives them "word attack skills". This means that when they read a word that they do not recognise they can break it into sections and by pronouncing each section can "build up" the word. For example, imagine a student trying to read this sentence:

At the zoo the boy saw a hippopotamus.

If the student does not recognise the word "hippopotamus" he breaks the word into sections such as:

hip-po-pot-a-mus

By pronouncing each section separately, he can build up the sound of the word "hippopotamus" and is able to understand the word hippopotamus and hence the whole sentence.

This is one of the reasons why spelling skills are often taught using a phonetic strategy, however it does not suit all students.

Most students, having learned how to spell words using a phonetic strategy, progress naturally to identifying words by sight i.e. by using their visual memory. People who do not have a reading difficulty do not use a phonetic strategy to read. As you are reading this chapter, are you reading each word by the phonetic sound or are you reading because you can visually identify each word easily? It seems that, after we learn to spell a word by using a phonetic strategy, our brain automatically converts the memory from an auditory memory to a visual memory.

The following words are "new" words if you are over the age of 25. (These words did not exist 25 years ago, in everyday language!)

e-mail

Internet

Word processing

Spreadsheet

Database

An average reader easily identifies these "new" words, even though they have not been learned initially using a phonetic strategy. We may have learned to spell in school using a phonetic strategy but most of us have since abandoned it in favour of a visual strategy for learning words. It seems that the phonetic strategy for learning spellings is a useful starting point for most people learning to spell. However, it is not necessarily suitable for all students and especially not for some students who have dyslexia.

A phonetic strategy depends on reading the word in context as a word spelt in identical form may sound different and have different meanings.

Demonstration:

Read the following sentences and notice the same spellings but different meanings and yet your brain is able to sort these out by looking at the words in context.

I was too *close* to the door to *close* it.

After a *number* of injections my jaw got *number.*

I had to *subject* the *subject* to a series of tests.

Upon seeing the *tear* in the painting I shed a *tear.*

The bandage was *wound* around the *wound.*

The farm was used to *produce produce.*

The dump was so full that it had to *refuse* more *refuse.*

We must *polish* the *Polish* furniture.

How can I *intimate* this to my most *intimate* friend?

He could *lead* if he would get the *lead* out.

When shot at, the *dove dove* into the bushes.

I did not *object* to the *object.*

The insurance was *invalid* for the *invalid.*

There was a *row* among the oarsmen about how to *row.*

The buck *does* funny things when the *does* are present.

A seamstress and a *sewer* fell down into a *sewer* line.

The soldier decided to *desert* his *dessert* in the *desert.*

To help with planting, the farmer taught his *sow* to *sow.*

The *wind* was too strong to *wind* the sail

Since there is no time like the *present*, he thought it was time to *present* the *present.*

(Author: *Unknown*)

Some of the above sentences are easier than others due to the closeness of the two ambiguous words within the sentence and others due to grammar whilst others are more common in everyday use. Some students with dyslexia only read one word at a time and thus find it difficult to sort meaning by context.

Why does a phonetic spelling strategy not suit all students?

If a student is severely colour-blind, he has a physical reason why he cannot recognise all the colours and this is a simple concept, which most people readily understand. We would not try to teach a colour-blind person all of the colours, as we would understand the difficulty and the impossibility from the student's point of view. If we were to try to teach all the colours to a colour-blind student we would fully understand his frustration. Imagine how great that frustration would be if this teaching were continued over a period of weeks, months and years.

In the same way that colour-blind students are unable to learn all the colours, some students with dyslexia have severe difficulty learning the sounds of a word and linking these sounds to the visual spelling of the word. Parents and teachers have been aware of this difficulty for some students for quite some time.

Until relatively recently, cognitive psychologists were of the view that dyslexia is a specific disability that affects only reading and writing, not speech or hearing, because generally students with dyslexia are able to communicate well orally. A major breakthrough in understanding dyslexia occurred when it was accepted that people with dyslexia often have subtle hearing difficulties. One particular difficulty often found is the inability to separate a word into its individual phonemes, or sounds, if these follow each other too rapidly.

Research currently being carried out by Dr. John Gabrieli and Dr. Torlel Klinberg at Stanford University suggests that this difficulty may be connected with the speed at which the sound signals are transmitted along the nerve fibres. If the signals travel too slowly they may crowd into each other with the result that the brain cannot process them correctly. The research is examining the physical causes of this problem and it seems possible that inadequate myelin insulation of nerve fibres may be involved. When two groups of adults, with and without dyslexia, were given a standardised reading test, DTI scans of their brains indicated that there was a difference between the two groups in the degree of myelination in the temporoparietal region of the brain's left hemisphere. This is the section of the brain that seems to control most language processing.

If the problem of recognising the sound of individual sections of a word such as hippopotamus above is indeed a physical problem, or a cognitive problem, then a different method of learning to spell is essential for individuals with this particular problem.

If a student with dyslexia has difficulty splitting up words into phonemes, or sounds, then he cannot start to learn to spell by using a phonetic strategy and it seems that such a student may also have difficulty progressing naturally to a visual strategy as other students do.

The dyslexia@bay™ System enables a student with dyslexia who has this problem to bypass the phonetic strategy, which he finds so difficult, and progress directly to a visual strategy for learning spellings. Not only will the student then have an effective strategy for learning spellings but also, by using his long-term visual memory rather than his short-term auditory memory, he will be able to remember the spellings he has learned in the long-term. Another major advantage of using a visual strategy is that students learn to identify words more easily when they are reading and hence learn to spell new words as they read. This may seem strange and yet this is the way that most of us learn new spellings.

How do most people who do not have a learning difficulty learn to spell new words?

We are able to identify the "new" words listed above because we have read them several times and learned to spell them using an unconscious visual strategy. If you think this is strange, try the following demonstrations.

Demonstration:

Think of some everyday groceries that you use, perhaps a particular breakfast cereal, a particular jar of coffee, a particular packet of pasta or a particular carton of soup. As you think of this particular foodstuff, think of the packaging and you will remember the colours, the shape, the size and most importantly the name. Stop reading at this point and make a picture in your mind of the particular foodstuff in its packaging. Examine the picture in your mind for colours, shape and size and look at the name on the packaging.

When you have done this ask yourself whether you learned to spell the name phonetically by sounding it out or visually by seeing it on a regular basis?

Demonstration:

Look at these words

excelent   *wunderful*   *magnifisent*

They "do not look right" do they? No they "look wrong". Yet these words are spelt correctly using a phonetic strategy. These words do not "look right" because our visual memory recognises that these words are spelt differently from the memory it has stored of the correct spelling. It is the visual memory of the spelling, which allows us to remember how to spell words in the long-term.

Why do people, when asked to spell an uncommon word, write down the word to see if the spelling "looks right"?

When asked to spell a word, not commonly used, we usually like to write the word down. We do this to visually examine the word and compare it to the word stored in our visual memory. If the spelling of the word written on the paper is the same as the spelling of the word in our visual memory, then we get a "feeling" that the spelling is correct. The opposite is also true if the spelling written on the paper is not the same as the spelling of the word in our visual memory. We get a "feeling" that the spelling does not look right and we change the order of letters, or insert some new letters or delete some letters until we get a "feeling" that we see the correct spelling. The spelling of the word on paper now concurs with our visual memory of the word, which we have probably remembered by reading the word several times.

Demonstration:

Take a pen and paper and write down some words leaving out one or two letters. Write down some other words mixing up the order of the letters and a few more adding in some extra letters.

You will now understand that you are remembering the look of the words in your visual memory rather than the sound of words in your auditory memory.

In conclusion, learning to spell using a phonetic strategy is a suitable starting point for most students who will progress naturally to a visual strategy to learn the correct spelling of words. Using a phonetic strategy seems to be an intermediary stage, or a stepping-stone, on the way to developing a visual strategy for spelling. However, if the student has difficulty using a phonetic strategy this intermediary stage is not available and hence the student has difficulty learning to spell. By using a "visual spelling programme", having first developed his visual memory, the student is able to bypass the phonetic stage and progress directly to a visual strategy. This enables him to learn spellings in the long-term as well as in the short-term and, over a period of time using this programme, the student also learns to use the correct spellings for words when writing stories and can more easily recognise words when reading etc.

Using phonics is easy isn't it?

It is easy for some but not others.

Eye have a spelling chequer
It came with my pea sea
It plainly marques four my revue
Miss steaks eye kin sea.

Eye strike a key and type a word
And weight four it two say
Weather eye am wrong oar write
It shows me straight a weigh.

As soon as a mist steak is maid
It nose bee fore two long
And eye can put the error rite
Its rare lea ever wrong.

Eye have run this poem threw it
I am sore your pleased two no
Its letter perfect awl the weigh
My chequer tolled me sew.

(Author: *Unknown*)

Chapter 5

Eye-tracking problems and implications

It is estimated that over 80% of information that is transmitted to the brain during academic learning is transmitted visually i.e. by use of our eyes. It is therefore essential for efficient and effective learning to take place that our eyes are functioning well. This goes beyond establishing that there are no refractive problems, such as shortsightedness, or pathological problems (disease), which would be identified in a standard eyesight test.

Reading is a complex visual task and requires good vision not just good eyesight. For example, both eyes have to work together as a team and converge equally in order to focus on the words being read which, incidentally, are generally about 16 inches from the eyes, not the 20 feet used in a standard eyesight test. The eyes have to be able to focus on more than a few letters at the same time to be able to read longer words easily. The eyes also have to be able to track across a page line-by-line and from left to right without skipping lines or reading lines twice. Difficulties associated with several different eye-tracking problems are discussed below.

What are the symptoms of eye-tracking problems?

Needing to run a finger underneath the line when reading.

Reading the same line again or skipping lines.

Losing "concentration" after a short time while reading a book.

Guessing the letters at the end of words.

Having tired eyes.

The words appearing to be blurred.

The words seeming to float around.

Needing to rub the eyes after reading for a period of time.

Difficulty copying words from the black/white board.

Needing to close one eye when reading (Voluntary Occlusion).

Feeling slightly queasy when reading for a period of time.

These are all signs of a student who has an eye-tracking difficulty
A student may have one or two of the above signs but is most unlikely to
have them all.

Catching a ball seems quite a simple task for most of us but we all know people who find it difficult. We say that they have little, or no, "co-ordination". When you consider it, catching a ball it is very complex skill. Both eyes have to be working in a co-ordinated fashion so that they can judge the speed of the ball, by estimating the distance the ball is from you several times, over a very short period of time. The brain then has to send a signal through the arm muscles and hand muscles to work in co-ordination to "catch the ball". There are many muscles in the arms and more in the hands. If any one of those muscles in the arms or hands were damaged, or not working in co-ordination with the other muscles, then you would be unable to catch the ball. This does not even taken into consideration the very delicate muscles that control your eyes, which are the muscles used to estimate the distance that the ball is from you.

Having considered the complexities involved in catching a ball it is really amazing that the human body can do it. We tend to take such a simple skill for granted.

Demonstration:

Have somebody throw a ball to you three times from a distance of one, two and three metres. Repeat the three catches first with your right-eye closed and then with your left-eye closed.

Your eyes need to be co-ordinated to measure the distance and, if you are only using one eye, you will not be able to measure distance accurately.

Co-ordinated eyes are necessary to catch a ball! *(See Chapter 11 for a more detailed discussion on how we judge distance.)*

In the same way, we tend to consider the skill of moving our eyes across lines of words on a page as a simple task. It is a natural skill for most people but not for everyone. Co-ordinated eyes are necessary to read!

Studies by Oxford University's Physiology Department found "Patching one eye can improve eye control and reading in dyslexic children with poor eye control." However this may solve the problem in the short term, as it removes the need for the eyes to be co-ordinated, but can be disadvantageous in the long term.

Why can my child read small words but have difficulty with longer words?

Each of our eyes has a field of vision and the area where the two fields of vision overlap is the where we see words when we are reading. In simplistic terms, if the overlap is small then we will be able to see only small words, whereas if it is large, we will be able to read large words.

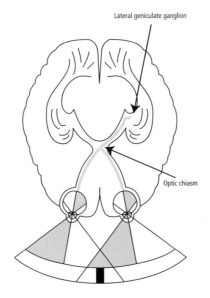

Diagram 5.1 Vision in an Integrated State

Some people with reading difficulties may have a small area of overlap. These people are relatively content to read a passage, which contains only small words. However, when challenged to read a passage with longer words then one of the following occurs. They may just stop reading when they come across longer words. They will be confused and have little comprehension of what they are reading. The other possibility is that they will continue to read but will guess the ends of words e.g. the following words all begin with th:, those, there, their, through.

The following sentence

The man bought those apples.

could be read in the following different ways:

The man bought there apples.

The man bought their apples.

The man bought through apples.

The first two sentences cause confusion, whereas the third sentence does not make any sense at all.

We refer to the size of a word, i.e. the numbers of letters it contains, as the "**chunk size**". As children get older and read longer words then we say that the chunk size is increasing. When we choose reading material for a child of a certain age we consider two things. First, we consider the degree of comprehension required to follow the story and second, the vocabulary, in particular the length of the words. How often have we said "that is a very big word for someone your age to know"?

If a child has difficulty understanding material, which is apparently age appropriate, it may be that he has a small chunk size rather than that he has a problem with comprehension. Very often these children have a very wide spoken vocabulary and yet seem to have difficulty reading books considered suitable for their age.

Demonstration:

Take a piece of paper and cut a hole in it that is wide enough to hold only five letters and read the preceding paragraph. Your degree of comprehension will be greatly reduced but, more importantly, you will understand how someone with a small chunk size reads.

Why does my child read some words backwards e.g. "no" for "on", "was" for "saw"?

We all have a dominant hand and foot i.e. most people are right-handed and right-footed although some people are left-handed and/or left-footed. Some people are considered to be ambidextrous because they are very skilful with both hands but, even so, one of the hands will be dominant.

In the same way, we all have a dominant or preferred "**direction of processing**" although the degree of dominance varies from person to person. When walking through a forest, most people who are right-handed will tend to brush the branches aside sweeping their right hand from left to right (vice versa for people who are left-handed). However, not all right-handed people will have a dominant direction of processing from left to right (vice versa for left-handed people).

In ancient Greece words were written along a line from left to right and the subsequent line was written right to left and so on in a zigzag fashion. Most languages nowadays, apart from in the Middle East, are written from left to right. Most people prefer to process from left to right but people who naturally process from right to left will seemingly read words backwards i.e. will read "was" for "saw" etc. This occurs only for words that can be read backwards. Some people in education are of the opinion that this is where the term "backward children" came from.

Why does my normally bright child find it difficult to remember which is left and which is right?

Parents are very often bewildered as to why their children continue to find it difficult to remember left and right. It is quite common for a young child to be confused between left and right and to use memory aids to help him remember. He may remember that he writes with his right hand and then simply decides if something is on the same side as the hand he writes with or not – he may remember that he kicks a football with his right foot or wears his watch on his left wrist. This is quite normal but what is not quite so normal is the continued use of such aids over a period of years.

Children with dyslexia are often confused between left and right and many of them will continue to use a memory aid. The problem is not the inability to remember the label of left and right but the inability to sense the left hand side and the right hand side. In other words the vertical midline is not well defined in their personal space and we call this **"horizontal or lateral confusion"**. It is very difficult to label something that you are unaware of and much more difficult to remember that label!

Demonstration:

Stand in the middle of a room and decide whether the door is on your left hand side or your right hand side. Close your eyes and turn round slowly several times in a clockwise direction and then several times in an anti-clockwise direction. Without opening your eyes decide if the door is on your left hand side or your right hand side. Now you will understand what is like to be confused by sidedness!

The reason that this confusion arises is that you have lost your sense of the relationship between your vertical midline and the room around you. People who are confused between left and right are often unaware of the relationship between their midline and their surroundings. If a student has this problem, it is paramount that it is addressed soon as possible.

Why does my child often read the same line again or skip lines when he is reading?

A child who has a preference for right to left processing may find that he tends to read the same line twice. He may also tend to skip lines by consciously trying to avoid reading the same line twice, by consciously casting his eyes on the line below. However he may cast his eyes downward too much and actually read the line two lines below. If the reader is a mechanical reader he may be totally unaware of what he has done. There are other reasons why a child may skip lines when reading and one of which may be that he has **"vertical confusion"** which is explained below.

Why does my child often "lose his place" when he is reading?

When reading a book, some people have great difficulty finding their place again if they are distracted and look away from the book for a short while. This is noticeable as the child's head may be seen to give a slight wobble as they seek the spot on the page to continue reading. They may put their finger on the last word they have read to keep their place. Without such a strategy they may return to the beginning of the page or paragraph that they have been reading. Such people suffer from **"vertical confusion"**.

Vertical confusion. In the same way that some people are confused between left and right (horizontal or lateral confusion) they may also be confused between up and down, above and below (vertical confusion). As well as a vertical midline we also have a horizontal midline running horizontally through our eyes. Some people do not have a well-defined sense of this horizontal midline in relation to their surroundings. Consequently, they will have difficulty in perceiving whether something is up or down, above or below the line of their eyes. It is easy to appreciate how this can lead to a child skipping lines when reading or not being able to find their place again when distracted from reading a book.

Demonstration:

Stand in a room and look at a shelf with objects sitting on it so that the shelf is level with your eyes. Look at an object on the left hand side and another object on the right hand side of the shelf and decide whether the objects are "above" or "below". Next tilt your head at an angle of about 45 degrees to the right hand side. Now decide if the object on the right hand side of the shelf is above or below. Next decide if the object on the left hand side of the shelf is above or below. Carry out exactly the same procedure only this time tilt your head to the left hand side. Decide if there is the same degree of confusion tilting your head either way.

For most people there will be a slight perceptual difference in the degree of confusion as the dominant eye should be the eye that calibrates "above" and "below".

Why does my child have difficulty copying a list of words accurately from the blackboard into his exercise book?

Children who experience **vertical confusion** will find it more difficult to copy a list of words from the blackboard into his exercise book. Imagine a child taking down the following list of words:-

dog

cat

camel

elephant

tiger

hippopotamus

The child may write the first two words accurately but then write "camel" as "catel", "elephant" as "elemhant" or "tiger" as "tiher". This causes great confusion for parents and teachers, as they cannot understand where the student discovered the "t" sound in camel, the "m" sound in elephant or the "h" sound in tiger.

You can imagine that if you had a rifle with a telescopic sight then it would be a relatively easy task to line up the cross wires on the target and shoot accurately. However, if you were told that the horizontal cross wire was slightly wrong, and you observed that the rifle always shot above the target, you would compensate by putting the horizontal cross wire slightly below the target before firing. You would have a major problem trying to hit the target if, each time you were to take aim, the horizontal cross wire changed position. This is what happens to someone who has vertical confusion. This is why, when they copy down the words, they place inappropriate letters from the words above or below into the word they are writing.

In the above case the child has taken the "t" from "cat" and put it into "camel" and the "m" from the word "camel" and placed it in the middle of "elephant". Similarly the "h" from "elephant" has been put into "tiger". The reason why the child cannot recognise that the "t" is a totally inappropriate sound for "camel" is dealt with in Chapter 4 dealing with the phonetic strategy for spelling and auditory sequencing.

Many children find a solution for vertical confusion by copying down the first one or two words then looking down at the words they have written, (in this case "cat") and looking for it on the blackboard and then copying down the word below it, (in this case "camel") and so on. This is an aid, but it is not a solution to the problem for two reasons. Firstly, this solution is very time-consuming and the child will take longer to take the material down from the board. As a result the child will feel very conscious of being "slower" than the rest of the class. Secondly, to overcome this feeling of failure, the child will tend to rush when writing down the list and will become careless, which also has negative results.

The solution to the problems caused by confusion between left and right (horizontal confusion) and between up and down (vertical confusion) is to develop in the student a well-defined sense of his vertical midline and his horizontal midline in relation to his surroundings. This is a contributory method by which eye-tracking problems suffered by so many students with dyslexia may be dealt with.

What does it feel like to have an eye-tracking problem when reading?

There are many different types of eye-tracking problems but to experience what it is like to read with an eye-tracking problem carry out the following demonstration.

Demonstration:

Take an ordinary paperback book and start reading it as normal. After the first paragraph, move the book from side to side slowly, about an inch at a time, and continue reading for two or three paragraphs keeping the movement going. That is what it feels like if you have horizontal confusion.

Next, continue reading without moving the book for one paragraph and then start to move the book up and down slowly, about an inch at a time, and read for a further two or three paragraphs. This is what it is like to have vertical confusion.

Finally, read a paragraph normally and then, this time, move the book from side to side and up and down. Keep alternating these movements for the next three paragraphs. This is what it feels like to have horizontal and vertical confusion.

It is not easy to read for a long period of time without experiencing eyestrain if you have an eye-tracking problem. In severe cases the child may feel queasy in the tummy and complain that he feels "sick" when reading.

If you look again at the list of signs of eye-tracking problems at the beginning of this chapter, you will now be much more aware of the reasons why such problems occur.

Why does my child lose concentration after reading for a period of time?

If you have carried out the above demonstration successfully, you will be able to sympathise with a child who has an eye-tracking problem. Moving the book from side to side, or up and down, or both does cause eyestrain. When a child is reading and suffering from such eyestrain, he will inevitably look up from the book and look around the room at distant objects to relieve the strain. A parent or teacher may interpret such behaviour as losing concentration, whereas in fact the child is merely relieving eyestrain.

In the next Chapter, you will discover how eye-tracking difficulties can affect the level of comprehension a child has when reading.

Chapter 6

How do we understand and remember what we read?

It is essential to recognise the paramount importance of comprehension when we read. There is little point in just being able to de-code the words on the page without being able to understand what the words, sentences, paragraphs and chapters mean. There would be no pleasure or purpose in reading and boredom and frustration would be inevitable. Furthermore, if we do not understand what we read, remembering what we read becomes so much more difficult.

What are the four main stages in reading?

1 Track our eyes across the lines of words on the page, from left to right and line-by-line.

2 Recognise the words in isolation and then as a group.

3 Say the words inside our head with our own internal voice.

4 Make an internal representation of what we are reading which, for most of us, is making a video or pictures in our head.

The last stage is the key to comprehension, which is to say to a full understanding and appreciation of what we have read.

As reading skills develop, most of us bypass the third stage which leads to considerably increased reading speeds.

How do eye-tracking difficulties affect comprehension?

The first stage in the process of reading is to track our eyes across the lines of words on the page, from left to right and line-by-line, and in Chapter 5 we discussed how some eye-tracking problems could arise. We will now look specifically at how eye-tracking problems affect comprehension.

35

If a child has an eye-tracking problem a large amount of concentration is used just to track the eyes across the lines of words and make an effort to recognise those words. There is a limited amount of concentration left for the child even to say the words inside his head let alone make a picture or video so that he understands what he has read. Without understanding, concentration will decrease still further.

This is why a person with dyslexia who also has an eye- tracking problem will have limited comprehension and memory of what they have just read.

Demonstration:

Find a descriptive passage in a novel and read it. Put the book down and recall the details of the passage.

The method you use to do this, albeit unconsciously, is to describe the picture or video you made in your head whilst reading the passage. The more details you have in the picture or video in your head, the greater will be your degree of comprehension and recall.

Some people make very detailed pictures or videos in their head and sometimes the videos will have associated sounds, voices and atmosphere. A reader who has a particularly vivid imagination will use "special effects" to add to the atmosphere of a story. The imagination of the human mind knows no bounds! It is limitless and this is probably the reason why people complain, when they watch the film of a book they have read, that "the film was not as good as the book!" When we read a book, we are our own movie director and that is why everyone interprets the same book in so many different ways. That is why, when we discuss with our friends a book we have read, we get so many different views. This perhaps is the main joy of reading, providing material with which our imagination can play.

Students with an eye-tracking problem are so often denied the opportunity to make these wonderful pictures and movies in their heads because they have to expend so much energy just de-coding the words.

What is mechanical reading?

A person who reads without comprehension is termed a "mechanical reader". Many of the people who have an eye-tracking problem are mechanical readers to some degree and do not make a visual representation in their head when they read. However, this is not the only reason why people are mechanical readers.

Once we have learned to read and, at the same time, make a picture of the story in our heads it is impossible not to do so. However, the following demonstration, whilst being quite difficult, is not impossible and gives great insight into how a mechanical reader reads.

Demonstration:

Find a descriptive passage in a novel but, before starting to read it, make a picture in your head of a place you know that gives you great pleasure. It could be somewhere you were on holiday, a particular Christmas Day as a child or a room in the house you grew up in of which you were particularly fond. Make the picture really vivid with lots of colour. Keep this picture in your mind and at the same time read the descriptive passage. You may find that your mind will wander and want to make a picture of the material you are reading. Try to concentrate on the picture of the place that gave you great pleasure.

At the end of the passage you may be amazed how little you remember of the passage you have just read.

Demonstration:

Please read the following:

Wind revolver about saddle then wispy hills wastepaper under special, potatoes rudder icecap television tissues although name underneath impossible mountain track paper and reverse steel almighty.

It doesn't make sense, does it? You can recognise the words easily, decode the words, understand the words and say them to yourself. The trouble arises when trying to do step 4, make an internal visual representation of your internal dialogue.

Welcome to the world of the mechanical reader!

By making the picture of the place that gives you great pleasure you actually blocked out the ability to make a picture in your head of what you were reading. This has the same effect as not actually being able to make a visual interpretation and you experienced what it is like to be a mechanical reader.

Why do some people read in a monotone and disregard punctuation?

This is related to the mechanical reader and occurs for the same reason. If a person is reading mechanically, that is to say merely de-coding the words and not making any visual representation in their head, they will have no understanding of what they are reading and consequently are not likely to read with any expression. By and large, punctuation is there to aid comprehension and so, if a person has little or no comprehension, the punctuation appears irrelevant.

This is perhaps best illustrated by the punctuation, which is used to identify when people are speaking. There may be several different characters in a story and the punctuation enables us to use different voices for the different characters thereby adding more detail to our videos and increasing our understanding. We may also choose to vary the speed, accent and tone with which the characters speak.

Demonstration:

Find a passage, about a page long, in a novel where two or three people are talking to each other. Place an audiocassette tape recorder beside you. Make the same picture that gave you great pleasure in your head as in the previous demonstration and take time to construct it properly. Keeping this picture in your head, read the passage out loud and record yourself.

Next, read the same passage out loud again and record yourself but this time make pictures of the characters in your head and add intonation to each character's voice.

Listen to the difference in your voice in the two recordings. Have you paid equal attention to punctuation in each reading session? Now you will understand why mechanical readers read with very little intonation or expression in their voice and ignore punctuation.

The reverse is that, when they write a story, they also leave out punctuation. When someone who has been labelled as having dyslexia writes a story, a possible characteristic is a lack of paragraphs and punctuation. Now that you have carried out the above demonstrations you will understand why.

Why does my child complain that reading is boring and yet enjoys a book being read to him?

If a child complains that reading is boring, despite the parent selecting reading material that they know the child would be interested in, it causes great confusion and frustration for the parent. Eye-tracking problems may provide an explanation in some cases.

If a child has an eye-tracking problem, he is unlikely to make a visual interpretation when he is reading to himself. As a result he will have little or no comprehension of what he is reading and will inevitably find it boring. On the other hand, if the story is being read to him, the eye-tracking difficulty is side stepped, he is free to make wonderful pictures and movies in his head and become absorbed in the story.

The visual interpretation we make when we read is different for each of us. Some people make photographs or still pictures in their head whereas others make movies or a video. Some readers make black-and-white pictures whilst others use vivid colour. Some people make large pictures in their heads whilst others make small pictures. Some people see two-dimensional pictures whilst others see pictures in three dimensions. These are some of the variations but by no means all. However, if a child has an eye-tracking problem then it is difficult for them to make any degree of interesting picture in their head when they are reading.

39

Demonstration:

Imagine watching an exciting video such as "Titanic" on the television and, half way through, someone turns the brightness on the screen down until the picture disappears and you can only hear the sound. How long would you continue to watch the video? Not long, I would suggest, in fact, you would probably become bored, stop watching and perhaps even turn the television off.

When we read a book, it is important for most of us to have the visual picture in our head much in the same way as watching a video. If we cannot see the picture in our head then we too would become bored.

Chapter 7

Difficulties associated with written work

Why do students with dyslexia often produce written work that is inconsistent with their oral ability?

There are two main aspects of the written work of students with dyslexia, which can be inconsistent with oral skills: -

(a) Their written essays and stories often lack sequence or appear to be 'mixed up' and often do not keep to the point. Orally they may well be able to present the same information convincingly and logically.

(b) Their essays and stories lack the vivid description and feeling which is often there when the student is telling a story orally.

What exactly do we mean by 'sequence' in written work?

In the next chapter, we will look more in more detail at sequencing but to appreciate what we mean by sequence in written work carry out the following demonstration.

Demonstration:

Imagine being asked to write an essay about your activities last weekend. Take a minute or two and reflect on what events happened during your last weekend; select about five of them. Take your time and sort the events systematically and in sequence according to time.

You should then be able to write a logical, chronological essay about the five events, which happened last weekend – your essay will be 'in sequence'.

So how exactly does your brain do this? What are the mental processes involved?

Explanation:

To order the five events according to time, you probably made pictures of the events in your mind, either imagining the picture as viewed through your own eyes or imagining seeing yourself in the picture. There are many different types of pictures that we can have in our mind. We can either view the picture of an event from the seat in the audience of a theatre, as if it was happening on the stage, or we can view the picture as if we ourselves were on the stage as it were in the middle of the picture. Some people view an event as if they were in helicopter looking down on the event happening below them.

The pictures may be still pictures as in a photograph or moving pictures as in a film or video *(See Chapter 16 for more detail)*. As you will see below, if the pictures you make are still pictures then you may not be able to sequence the events correctly - moving pictures are the key to correct sequencing.

If we see the events as a series of still photographs then we could imagine laying these photographs in a line on a table. If we were to number these photographs 1 to 5, then we could say that the photographs were in sequence.

1 2 3 4 5

It is relatively easy however to move the second photograph to the position of the third photograph and the first photograph to the end. The photographs would then be ordered as follows: -

3 2 4 5 1

which, of course, is not in sequence.

Why does the written work of children with dyslexia often lack sequence?

Example:

Imagine a young child is asked to write an essay about what he did last Sunday. The actual order of events may have been as follows:

Got out of bed and had breakfast with the family.

Assembled his football gear and went and played a football match.

Came home and had lunch.

Went with the family to see a film in the cinema.

Came home, had dinner and watched television.

However, if the child has dyslexia he may not be able to make moving pictures and may not be able to arrange the still pictures of the events he makes in his mind in the correct order. Consequently, he may write the essay in the following sequence:

3. Came home and had lunch.

2. Assembled his football gear and went and played a football match.

4. Went with the family to see a film in the cinema.

5. Came home, had dinner and watched television.

1. Got out of bed and had breakfast with the family.

This of course is an exaggerated example but it does illustrate why a student with dyslexia might write a non-sequential essay. Equally because the student feels that the essay is not quite in the right order he may well become distracted and hence punctuation, spellings and other grammatical syntax will suffer further.

Also, as they are processing using individual still photographs and therefore not seeing the "whole picture", there may be a tendency to go off on a tangent and deviate from the "main story" or inappropriately write about one section of the essay.

How do children without dyslexia write essays that are in sequence and not mixed up?

Most children, when asked to write an essay, imagine the events happening in a film or video – they make moving pictures. Once a series of events is thought of as a video then the sequence of events is "locked in". The events follow each other in sequence and are not so easily re-arranged. When these children are asked to write about something from memory, such as what they did last Sunday, they 'play the video' in their mind and write from the video.

Why are some students with dyslexia great at telling stories orally with plenty of description and feeling, but yet this is not transferred to their written work?

Demonstration:

Return to the demonstration at the beginning of this Chapter and this time organise the events according to how significant the events were and/or how much you enjoyed them.

The events you chose were most likely those, which were either out of the ordinary, or those, which gave you most enjoyment or hassle.

The pictures you made in your mind to organise the events, as well as being still or moving, may also have been constructed in one of two different ways. You may have imagined the pictures as viewed through your own eyes or you may have imagined seeing yourself in the pictures. The first way is rather like viewing the picture as if we ourselves were on a stage taking part in the event, whereas the second way is rather like viewing the picture of an event from a seat in the audience, as if the event were happening on the stage. For some people this second way is like viewing an event from above, rather like being in a helicopter and looking down on the event.

These are two very distinct types of visual memory. The first type of memory we have when we view the memory through our own eyes is referred to as an associated memory i.e. we are associated within our own body when viewing the memory and hence we are able to associate with the emotions of the memory. The second type of memory we have is when we view the memory from outside our own body i.e. dissociated from our body and this is termed a dissociated memory. As we are dissociated from our body in the memory we do not as readily identify with the emotions of the memory. Sometimes we remember an event in our lives when we were silly or embarrassed and we enjoy a laugh at ourselves. When we recall this type of memory we tend to visualise looking at ourselves from outside our own body. It is easier to dissociate ourselves from the silliness, or embarrassment, of the event and to see the humour involved, if we view the memory, not from within our body, but from outside our body at a distance.

When a child comes to an adult, feeling embarrassed, ashamed or angry, the adult may say something like "Don't be embarrassed, ashamed or angry. Imagine what other people will think, they will think it is just funny or silly; don't worry about it!" We hope the child will see the event in a new perspective and laugh at himself and stop feeling negative about the event.

What has happened? When the child explains what has happened to the adult he will be associated into the memory and into the emotions of embarrassment, shame or anger. He will be re-living the experience through his own eyes. The adult has encouraged the child to view the event as others might see it i.e. encouraged the child to view what has happened from outside of himself and thus to dissociate himself from the negative emotions involved in the memory.

As an adult, it is so easy for us to reflect upon events in our adolescent childhood and wonder why we were so emotionally involved at the time!

Demonstration:

Remember back to the past when you had a favourite toy that you felt very attached to. It may be a teddy bear or doll that was treated as a real life person or companion. The toy may be a bicycle, which you were very proud of and enjoyed cycling to "special places". The toy may have been toy pots and pans with which you cooked endless meals using sweets instead of normal groceries as ingredients. After you have remembered that "special toy", remember a particular place where you played with the toy, maybe by yourself or with others. Imagine you are back at that young age and you can feel the weight of the toy in your hands and you can feel the shape and colour of the toy. In fact, as you remember the details of the toy you can probably imagine the good emotions you felt, as the child playing with that toy. Take time and relive the pleasure you had playing with the special toy.

As you have this memory, you are looking at the toy from within your own eyes as a child and are associated into the good feelings of the memory of that special toy. As you remember playing with that toy you are probably making a "video" in your mind. Imagine taking a pencil and paper in your hand and writing down a description of the toy, where you played with the toy, with whom you played with the toy either by yourself or with others. You can probably easily remember the emotions of laughter and joy when playing with the toy and probably even one special occasion.

Take a moment or two and think of a few sentences that you would write to describe the toy and the special moments of happiness you had and the emotions involved.

Next imagine being in helicopter, looking down at the younger you playing with the toy. Looking down you can still see all the details of the toy and the surroundings, and perhaps others in the scene. You can also see how you looked as a child. This can be quite an amusing process but notice that you are now imagining the memory not through your own eyes as a child but from outside your body as a child. The term for this is a dissociated memory. Notice that when you remember the memory from this dissociated state then you do not feel the emotions you felt as the child. To regain the emotions you must imagine you are inside your own body as a child.

What is the significance of using visual memory either in associated or dissociated form? As noted above, when we are associated within a memory we feel the emotions and hence if we describe the memory we will use emotional and vividly descriptive language. However, if we are dissociated from the memory, we do not identify with the emotions or the vividness of the memory and hence we will not use emotional or vividly descriptive language and anyone reading the account will say the account is dry or not very imaginative.

When a student with dyslexia is asked to describe an event orally then he can be totally associated into the memory, looking through his own eyes and describe the event in great detail. However, when asked to write down a description of the event, he may well then become dissociated and hence the details of the description are lost.

Why do some students with dyslexia read in a monotone whereas normally they have an animated voice?

Normally, when someone is re-counting an event such as describing a holiday they have been on, they are fully associated inside their own body, looking through their eyes and hence they are fully animated in feeling the emotions of the holiday.

Some students with dyslexia, however, when reading out loud about an event are totally dissociated from the image of the event, or perhaps do not make an image at all, and hence do not feel emotionally connected with the story and hence they read in a monotone.

Why do older students have difficulty analysing the most important points about a chapter of a book?

If students read out loud in a monotone then, when they are listening to themselves internally, that internal voice will also be in a monotone. The voice will not change in tone or speed.

When reading a chapter of a book to themselves, they are dissociated and purely reading a collection of words. They do not change the intonation of their internal voice to mark out the salient and important points in the chapter.

Chapter 8

Sequencing problems and their implications.

What exactly is sequencing?

To put events in sequence means to put them in order, in relation to time. Most people retire from work, go to school, are born, have a job in the workplace and learn to walk. These stages are obviously out of sequence. To put them in sequence we would rearrange them into, be born, learn to walk, go to school, have a job in the workplace and retire from work.

What difficulties arise for those students who have sequencing problems?

If someone experiences sequencing problems they are likely to have the following difficulties:

Inability to follow the plot of a book in a logical order.

Lack of awareness of how much time has passed.

Feeling overwhelmed when asked to do homework.

Being unable to follow a set of instructions in order and without omitting any.

The basic mechanics for the thought processes involved in sequencing depend upon visual memory - one of the three basic types of memory as discussed at the beginning of Chapter 4.

What are the different modes of memory?

As mentioned before, people use three basic memory modes: auditory, kinaesthetic (practical) and visual.

Auditory memory is used to remember the words of a song, a poem or a nursery rhyme. We can remember the words using our own voice or someone else's voice e.g. a song being sung by a particular singer or a nursery rhyme in a parent's voice etc.

Kinaesthetic (practical) memory is used when we remember how to do something with our body, e.g. the feeling of swinging a golf club or a tennis racket, kicking a football or casting a fishing rod.

Visual memory is used to remember a picture in our mind e.g. a place we have been, a face that we know or a house that we have visited. For some people, the picture they make in their mind is as if they were looking through their own eyes and we term this kind of visual memory, an associated memory. Other people construct the picture so that they see themselves in the picture. They are not looking through their own eyes and they perceive the visual memory as an out of body experience. This kind of visual memory is termed, a dissociated memory.

How exactly do we use our visual memory to sequence?

According to the dyslexia@bay™ model of the brain (Chapter 16), there are two basic types of visual memory - Visual Static Memory and Visual Dynamic Memory. Visual Static Memory is used when we remember still pictures such as a photograph or painting. Visual Dynamic Memory is used when we remember a series of events/pictures as a movie or video. It is important to appreciate the difference between these two types of visual memory to understand how sequencing problems can arise.

Demonstration:

Think of a holiday that you really enjoyed. Remember the place you stayed, how you travelled to that place, a particularly happy event on that holiday, the journey home, a particular meal and who was present at the meal and finally remember a particular place that you visited and why you enjoyed it so much. As you remember each of these memories make the picture in your mind as big as possible and in as much detail and colour as possible.

Next remember all the events in order: first how you travelled to the place and lastly the journey home, with the other events in order, in between the journey there and the journey home.

An interesting thing has happened - your mind has sorted these visual memories according to time – but how did it do that?

Explanation:

If you imagine each of the events from the holiday as a still photograph and imagine laying the photographs down side by side on a table, the order of the photographs can easily be changed. There is no inherent order, by time or otherwise. To put the photographs in time order, you have to review the whole holiday as a video in your mind, albeit at an unconscious level, and order the photographs according to the sequence in the video.

You imagine each event as a still photograph using your Visual Static Memory and then put them in order by converting them to a video using your Visual Dynamic Memory.

Visual Static Memory and Visual Dynamic Memory can be thought of as two distinct locations in our mind. In order to organise memories in our head according to time, it is important to take the memories from a Visual Static Memory location and put them in a Visual Dynamic Memory location. Most people do this everyday and many times each day. For example, when someone wants to tidy up a room or an office, first of all they make a picture in their mind of the room or office tidy. Next they think of the necessary steps as pictures in their head. Finally they organise the steps into a video and then simply follow the steps in the video in order.

Demonstration:

Think of a new task that you will have to do in the future that you have not done in the past. Make a picture in your mind of the task having been completed. Next, divide the task up into steps and make a picture of each step. Finally join the individual pictures together and make a video of the task from beginning to end.

Most people do this unconsciously, as a matter of routine and those who break the task into small sequential steps are those who are most logical and efficient and rarely have to "go over their work again".

Some people do not do this process at all because they seem to be unable to access their Visual Dynamic Memory. They can break a task into steps but they cannot put the steps into a logical sequence because they cannot transfer the steps from Visual Static Memory to Visual Dynamic Memory and hence tackle the task illogically.

Some students with dyslexia are unable to access their Visual Dynamic Memory and tackle tasks in a very haphazard fashion, frequently having to "go over their work again". This causes frustration and results in a lack of enthusiasm to tackle new tasks.

Demonstration:

Imagine being given the following instructions. First you are asked to mow the lawn. Next you are asked to trim a hedge beside the lawn with the result that the hedge clippings fall on to the newly mown lawn. The result of this is that you have to mow the lawn again if you want the lawn to look neat, tidy and newly mown! Can you imagine the frustration of having to go back over your work again?

This happens to people who cannot access their Visual Dynamic Memory. They can break a task into steps but they cannot put the steps into a logical sequence because they cannot transfer the steps from Visual Static Memory to Visual Dynamic Memory and hence are unable to tackle the task logically.

Why are some students with dyslexia unable to follow the plot of a story they are reading?

Students often have a reading book in school and are required to read a passage from the book each day. A student with dyslexia may remember the names of the characters and individual events but is often unable to follow the plot of the story unless it is explained to them. This puzzles both parents and teachers and gives rise to frustration for the student.

Demonstration:

Imagine you are going to watch a video that you have never seen before. Someone plays the video for you in two-minute sequences and not in order! You see a two-minute sequence from the beginning, a sequence from the end, a sequence from the middle, a sequence from the beginning, a sequence from near the end and so on. How easy would it be to follow the plot of the video?

Some students with dyslexia, who do not have an eye-tracking problem, do manage to make a visual representation of the passage that they are reading. However, their visual representation is rather like a series of still photographs which are stored in Visual Static Memory and do not transfer to Visual Dynamic Memory. Consequently, the student follows the story as a series of individual photographs, which may be out of sequence and do not form a continuous video. This is very similar to watching the video in the above demonstration in two-minute sequences, which are not in order. As a result, the student is unable to follow the plot of the story. I wonder how many people would read a book if they could not follow the plot? You can now understand the frustration of some students with dyslexia when asked the question "Do you not enjoy reading the story?"

This also explains why some people with dyslexia choose to read very short passages in magazines or comics that have associated pictures in the correct sequence. It also explains why they have difficulty progressing from reading books, which have associated pictures to reading books without pictures. It is not merely a question of making a picture in their mind but it must be a picture that is able to transfer from Visual Static Memory to Visual Dynamic Memory in order to make sense of the plot. If a student has this problem, it is a major consideration for him whether reading for pleasure, homework or in preparation for an exam.

Why do some students who have dyslexia have no sense of the amount of time passing?

Some students who have dyslexia seem to take a long time to carry out even a simple task but this may be due more to their having no sense of the amount of time, which has passed rather than actually being "slow". It is important to note that this is so only for some students with dyslexia and certainly not all.

How do we sense how much time has passed? If we carry out a series of tasks e.g. trim a hedge, weed a flowerbed and mow a lawn we are somehow aware of whether we are carrying out the tasks within an expected period of time or whether the tasks are taking a shorter or longer period of time than we "thought".

Demonstration:

Stand at one end of the room and walk from one side of the room to the other. Go back to the starting point and make a "video" in your head of walking across the room. Next double the speed of your "video" and then double the speed of that "video" again. Now run the "fast video" in your head and walk across the room at the same time.

Next return to the starting point and without walking, run the "normal video" in your head. Now halve the speed of the "video" and then halve the speed again. You now have a "slow video" of walking across the room in your head. Now run the "slow video" in your head and walk across the room at the same time.

What did you notice? Most people notice that the speed with which they run the video in their head determines the speed with which they walk across the room! It seems that our physiology responds to the speed of the dynamic visual representation of the action we make in our mind, before we actually perform that action.

Similarly, before we carry out a series of tasks we make, at an unconscious level, a video of carrying out those tasks. If we carry out the tasks at a quicker speed than the video we have prepared in our mind the tasks will seem to be completed quicker than we "thought". We usually decide that the tasks were easier than we expected. If we carry out the tasks at a slower speed than the video in our mind, then the tasks will seem to take too long to complete. We may then decide that we took too much time to complete the tasks and we may get slightly frustrated. Obviously, if we carry out the tasks at the same speed as the video in our mind then we say that the tasks took as long as we "thought".

If a student with dyslexia does not access their Visual Dynamic Memory it means that they do not make "videos" in their head. This explains why such students appear to have no sense of time! As a result, they can take inappropriately long periods of time to do tasks.

Why do students with dyslexia feel overwhelm when doing homework?

Most students when sitting down to do their homework are aware of the sequence in which they intend to do it e.g. sums first, then English writing, reading and tables. They make a video in their head and, as each part of their homework is finished, they have a sense of completion. They know when they are halfway through their homework, or nearly finished. Thus they have a sense of progress and can estimate how much time is left to complete their homework.

However, if a student with dyslexia cannot access their Visual Dynamic Memory it means they cannot make a video of doing their homework and hence cannot estimate when they are halfway through, three quarters of the way through or nearly finished. Parents and teachers often find it difficult to understand that the student does not feel any sense of completion. It is important to imagine the situation from the student's point of view.

Demonstration

Imagine you are given the following set of tasks to carry out: tidy up your workplace, go to the supermarket and buy the weekly groceries, buy a newspaper, collect the cleaning from the dry cleaners, clean and tidy up your home, wash the car, vacuum the inside of the car, polish the car, tidy up the garden and carry out all of the tasks in one day!

When asked to do this number of tasks in a relatively short period of time we suffer the feeling of "overwhelm". Overwhelm occurs when we have many tasks to do and a seemingly inappropriate amount of time to carry them out. Overwhelm is a negative emotion and certainly deprives us of a sense of enthusiasm for carrying out the tasks, which in turn makes us feel a lack of completion and even more overwhelm.

The student with dyslexia who experiences sequencing problems feels this same sense of overwhelm when sitting down to tackle their homework! They are incapable of making a video of doing their homework in sequence and this is why they feel overwhelm. If they have a negative attitude towards their homework due to overwhelm then the homework is not carried out as well as it could be. There is no sense of satisfaction in completing the work and certainly no sense of pride in the quality of the work, hence the feelings of dread of homework, which some students with dyslexia experience.

We all like to think that we enjoy a sense of " job satisfaction" in our work. Imagine what our job would feel like if we had no sense of "job satisfaction", or a feeling that our job was seemingly endless, or that we had no sense of completion, or that we had no enthusiasm to carry out the job, or that we had no pride in the job when completed. These are the emotions felt by a lot of students who have dyslexia.

Why does my child seem unable to follow a set of simple instructions?

Some parents are puzzled why their child seems unable to follow a simple set of instructions e.g. when asked to go to the bedroom to fetch their pyjamas and slippers, they seem to forget what they were sent for, or when sent to the shop to buy three or four items they return with only one or two. Very often when the child is asked to do a few simple tasks they become distracted and seemingly forget what they were asked to do.

Explanation:

When asked to do a list of simple tasks there are two ways to remember. The first is to say them to oneself and repeat the list. This is how we use auditory memory and it works quite efficiently if one has a good auditory memory. This is not the case with many students who have dyslexia because their auditory memory functions differently and less efficiently. When someone with dyslexia tries to use this method they are often unable to retrieve the set of instructions from their auditory memory. This is the reason why some children with dyslexia seem to "ignore" the instructions and get distracted by other things.

The other method that can be used to remember a set of instructions is to use visual memory and to make a video in your mind using Visual Dynamic Memory. This option is rarely fully available to someone with dyslexia.

What are the implications of being unable to follow a set of simple instructions?

The method used by a teacher when teaching a complex task such as "punctuation" is to break the complex task into simple steps and to teach each step systematically and in sequence. The student watches as the explanation of the task unfolds before them. By visually rehearsing the video of the explanation and then carrying out the steps in the video for themselves, the student learns how to carry out a complex task such as punctuation.

As we have seen, if the student with dyslexia cannot remember the set of instructions either by using auditory memory or Visual Dynamic Memory, then the task becomes almost impossible.

The above explanation should clarify why intelligent students with dyslexia can speak fluently on a very complex topic but yet seem unable to transfer the complexity of their thoughts on to paper. It can be a source of great puzzlement for parents that when they speak to the children they seem so intelligent and logical but that this is not manifested in the written work required of them in school. It also explains why it is much easier to identify students with dyslexia and above average ability.

Why are some students with dyslexia very good at mathematics, sometimes exceptionally brilliant?

There are many cases where children with dyslexia have difficulty reading, writing and spelling but are excellent at mathematics. It seems so strange to parents and teachers that some children with dyslexia have difficulty remembering spellings over a period of time and yet can remember mathematical tables easily.

Explanation:

When the student with dyslexia tries to remember spellings taught using a phonetic strategy, they are trying to remember spellings using their auditory memory. However, when these students "learn" mathematical tables they remember them using Visual Static Memory and hence can remember them easily.

These same students tend to do mathematics in a different way from most students. The majority of students will learn to do a mathematical problem in a logical and sequential manner step-by-step. Linear processing arrives at this type of solution.

The student with dyslexia, who is also good at mathematics, sometimes tends to do the mathematical problem as a whole and will write down very few lines to solve the problem. Thinking of several parts of the problem at the same time i.e. a thinking pattern that allows the mind to process several thoughts together arrives at this type of solution. Co-processing several parts of the problem together arrives at this type of solution. Very often when they are asked how did they get the answer, they will reply that they do not know how they got the answer but are absolutely convinced that the answer is correct. Interestingly enough, the answer is often the correct answer! This particular type of student with dyslexia will very often be "naturally good" at writing software for the computer industry. Unfortunately within the examination system marks are given for each step of a mathematical solution not just for the correct answer. The examination system can be less than generous when dealing with the student with dyslexia who solves mathematical problems in the above manner if the numerical answer is incorrect and he has not shown the steps of the method he used to solve the problem.

If a student has sequencing problems it is essential to first help to rectify the student's visual perception in such a way as to allow the student to be able to use Visual Dynamic Memory and hence be able to think logically and sequentially.

This will give the student a strategy to enable them to follow a set of instructions easily and methodically, to avoid the feeling of overwhelm when asked to do homework, to have a better sense of the time passing and to be able to follow the plot of a book. However if the student has a natural talent for co-processing then he can still choose to think in this manner which may be appropriate for solving complex mathematical problems for example when not in the exam room. The student is able to choose between both types of thinking!

Chapter 9

What is dominance and why is it important?

Each person has a dominant hand, foot, eye and ear. When we choose to write something with a pen we generally write with our dominant hand. We say that our dominant hand is the one we have most "control" over. In the same way we have a dominant foot, the one we use to kick a ball, but what is not generally known is that we also have a dominant ear and a dominant eye.

Demonstration:

Take a blank piece of paper and write your name and address on it with your dominant hand. Next write your name and address again only this time use your other hand. Some people are very dominant in one hand i.e. they find it very difficult to write with their non-dominant hand. Some people are ambidextrous that is to say, that they can do many tasks equally with both hands. However, when it comes to writing then one hand will usually be far superior at the skill of writing. You can look at your degree of dominance by comparing how you wrote your name and address with each hand.

Is it possible to have mixed dominance between the hand and the foot?

The simple answer is "yes", and the implications are important. When we use our dominant hand, which for most people is the right-hand, the left half of the brain manipulates it. It is the same for most functions of our body. When we move the toes of our left foot they are controlled by the right half of the brain. When we raise our right knee the left half of the brain is directing this movement.

We can now appreciate that if someone is right-hand dominant and left-foot dominant then there will be some confusion in the brain, as dominance is "mixed". It is easy to understand how some people who have mixed dominance could at times be clumsy.

How can I discover a person's dominant hand?

Approach someone and offer him/her an object e.g. a bunch of keys, a book, a pen. The hand with which they accept the object will be their dominant hand.

How can I discover a person's dominant foot?

Ask the person to stand with the toes and heels together. Now gently push them in the middle of the back until they start to lose balance. As they lose balance, they will move one foot forward so that they do not fall flat on their face. The foot that they move forward will be their dominant foot. Sometimes this procedure has to be repeated several times to ensure a correct result.

Is it possible to have mixed dominance between the hand and the ear?

Again the simple answer to this is "yes" and again the implications are important. If someone has a dominant right-ear and their method of learning is primarily auditory, then they should sit on the left-hand side of a room when listening to someone teaching. The sound waves produced as the teacher talks will have a more direct entry into the dominant ear. However, this is not the only consideration. We should also consider which hand is dominant.

Demonstration:

Take a blank sheet of paper and place it on the desk to your left-hand side by about 12 to 15 inches and write your name. Next take the same sheet of paper and place it at about 12 to 15 inches to your right-hand side and write your name.

It will be much more comfortable to write your name, when the paper is moved to the same side as your dominant hand. This is partly because of the mechanics of the bone structure of the hand and wrist but is also because we have a "mid-line". Imagine a line running from the middle of the head down the centre of the nose through the centre of the chest, down to a point between the feet. This would be the mid-line.

If you have a dominant right-hand, it is much easier to write your name when the paper is on the right-hand side of your mid-line. Hence, a person who is right-ear dominant and right-hand dominant will be more comfortable on the left side of the classroom than a person who is right-ear dominant and left-hand dominant because they will want to position the paper to the left of their mid-line.

How can I discover a person's dominant ear?

Ask someone to pretend that somebody is talking about him or her on the other side of a wall. Ask them to try to listen to what they are saying by putting their ear to the wall. The ear that they place next to the wall is their dominant ear.

If you wish to appreciate the implications of being on the "right" side of a room when listening try the following demonstration:

Demonstration:

Turn on a radio to low volume so that you can barely hear what is being said. Now step back three paces and try to listen to what is being talked about on the radio. You will find that you turn your dominant ear towards the radio. Next, turn your dominant ear away from the radio and notice how much more difficult it is to hear what is being said. Notice also how unnatural it is to try to listen with your dominant ear turned away from the radio. Now you will understand the significance of being on the correct side of a class room if you are an auditory learner.

Next time you are having a conversation with someone, notice if you do turn your dominant ear towards the other person slightly.

Remember, if you are right-hand dominant that hand is controlled by the left side of the brain and, in the same way, if you are right-ear dominant that ear is controlled by the left side of the brain.

How can I discover a person's dominant eye?

Take a blank sheet of paper about six inches by six inches and cut a small circular hole in the centre about a half an inch in diameter. Ask the person to take the piece of paper in their dominant hand and look through the hole at an object several feet away. Then ask them to gradually bring the piece of paper towards their face, all the time keeping the object in view. Notice which eye the paper came towards – this is their dominant eye.

What are the implications of knowing which is the dominant eye?

Demonstration:

Take a book and read a paragraph with the book in line with your mid-line. Without turning your head, move the book twelve inches to your left and read the next paragraph. Read the following paragraph with the book positioned about twelve inches to your right and again do not turn your head.

Most people carrying out this demonstration experience a degree of unease trying to find the next line to read, when the book is not in line with their mid-line.

However, some people will prefer to hold the book to one side or the other. For example, a person who is left-hand dominant and left-eye dominant may well choose to hold the book to their left. However, as you will see in Chapter 11 this may cause different problems because both eyes will not be in focus.

If a person has a dominant right-hand and wants to hold the book to the right side of the mid-line this can cause unease when reading if they have a dominant left-eye.

Demonstration:

Take a book and read the page on the left-hand side. When you have finished that page, read the page on the right-hand side. Notice what happens when you change from the left-hand page to the right-hand page.

If you are right-handed you may well have held the book in your right hand and slightly to the right of your mid-line.

When changing from reading the left-hand side to the right-hand side you may find that you move the book to the left or rotate the book to the right if you are right-eye dominant so that the text is just to the right of the mid-line.

However, mixed dominance as well as other factors may result in different observations.

Try this:

Observe people standing in a room having a conversation and notice that they very rarely stand exactly opposite to each other. Observe them closely and try to decide the dominant eye and dominant ear of each person.

Chapter 10

Problems associated with clockwise/anti-clockwise dominance

Why do some people have difficulty learning to tell the time?

Why are some students confused between b and d?

Why do some people write a 3 or a 6 backwards?

Why do some students write numbers and letters differently?

Why do some people have difficulty learning to tell the time?

Demonstration:

Put down the book for a moment and with your dominant hand draw a large circle (approximately two feet in diameter) in front of you. Next, draw the circle in the opposite direction.

Did you draw a clockwise circle or an anti-clockwise circle first? If you drew a clockwise circle first, then you are "clockwise dominant" and vice versa. Most right-handed people are clockwise dominant. The degree of dominance is measured by the difference in "comfort" when drawing circles in either direction. We can measure the "comfort" by comparing the size of the two circles and the speed with which they are drawn. For most people there is not much difference between drawing clockwise and anti-clockwise circles. However, for some people there is a considerable difference.

Clocks are designed so that the hands move in a clockwise direction because most people are either clockwise dominant or there is not much difference in their degree of dominance. However, if someone is strongly anti-clockwise dominant then they will have difficulty learning to tell the time. When a left-handed person goes to a restaurant they will usually find that the knife is laid on the right and the fork on the left. However, they can easily change the position of the knife and fork to suit them. Although it is possible to purchase a clock with the numbers in anti-clockwise order and it would be easier for someone who is anti-clockwise dominant to learn to tell the time with an anti-clockwise clock, this is of limited use, as the vast majority of clocks are clockwise.

Why do some children mix b's and d's?

There are several reasons why some children are confused between b and d, p and q. When this problem is associated with clockwise or anti-clockwise dominance then it may be due to writing the letter in an inappropriate way.

Demonstration:

With a pencil or pen draw the letter b and beside it draw a letter d.

When you drew the letter b you probably started with a vertical line and drew a clockwise semi-circle starting in the middle of the vertical line. When you drew the letter d you probably started with a vertical line again and drew an anti-clockwise semi-circle starting in the middle of the vertical line. Repeat the procedure with the letters p and q. By examining how you do this you will appreciate that b and p are clockwise letters whereas d and q are anti-clockwise letters.

If a student is clockwise dominant then he may draw the letter b normally but the letter d may be drawn so that the semi-circle is drawn from the bottom of the vertical line so that it also turns into a clockwise letter. (Vice versa for an anti-clockwise student). When we first learn to draw the letters b and d we "feel the difference" between the letters However, if we draw both letters either clockwise or anti-clockwise then we do not learn to "feel the difference" and therefore do not "know" the difference between b and d.

Clockwise - Anticlockwise   Dominant b's and d's

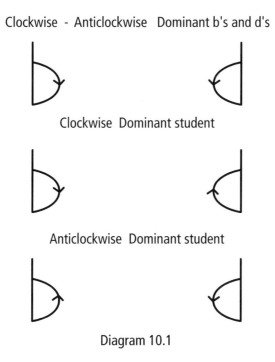

Clockwise Dominant student

Anticlockwise Dominant student

Diagram 10.1

Why do some people draw a 3 or a 6 or other numbers back to front?

Demonstration:

On a page draw the number 6 as a clockwise number and as an anti-clockwise number.

You should notice that for anti-clockwise, you start at the "top" of the number and draw the bottom circle as an anti-clockwise circle. When you draw 6 as a clockwise number you start from the middle and draw the circle as a clockwise circle and draw back up towards the top of the number 6.

If a student is clockwise dominant then he may draw the 6 as a clockwise number starting from the middle or he may draw it as a mirror image.

A student who is anti-clockwise dominant may draw the number 3 starting at the bottom rather than the top or as a mirror image. The same applies for other numbers and letters.

Why do some students write numbers and letters differently?

After you do this you will appreciate why some people draw the number 5 and other numbers and letters in a different way.

Demonstration:

Write the number 5 as an anti-clockwise number by starting at the bottom of the number and drawing upwards.

This will feel strange because you probably draw a 5 as a clockwise number normally, from the top, and the discomfort you feel is the same discomfort that an anti-clockwise dominant person feels when drawing a 5 as taught in school! Appreciate why some people write numbers and letters differently.

Demonstration:

Write down your full christian name and surname. Examine how many letters are clockwise and how many letters are anti-clockwise. Appreciate the difficulty experienced by those people who are strongly either clockwise or anti-clockwise dominant.

When we ask someone can they not "see the difference between b and d" we should now understand why they cannot "see the difference". Perhaps a more useful question would be "can you feel the difference between b and d" after making sure that they write the letter b clockwise and the letter d anti-clockwise!

Chapter 11

How do our eyes "see" words and letters and how does our brain process this visual information so that we can read?

As we have already mentioned in Chapter 5, over 80% of learning is estimated to take place visually. Visual information, in the form of written words, from books, handouts, notes, blackboard presentations, overhead acetates or computer screens enters the brain via the two eyes and is subsequently de-coded by the brain. This system relies on two distinct systems working correctly. Firstly, the eyes must work together to scan or track across the lines of words correctly, and secondly the visual pathway from the eyes to the brain must relay the information accurately. This is not always the case for people with dyslexia. If one or both systems are faulty, reading writing and spelling can be a struggle.

So exactly how do our eyes scan over the lines of words when we read and exactly how does the brain then de-code the information?

What is the significance of having eyes in the front of our head?

Most animals, (e.g. horses, dogs and cows) and most birds (other than birds of prey), have an eye on either side of their head (Diagram 11.1). In contrast, birds of prey, cats, monkeys and human beings have eyes at the front of their head.

Animals or birds that are more likely to be hunted than to hunt, usually have an eye on each side of their head giving them a wide visual field or what we call panoramic vision. Lateral placement of the eyes allows the animal

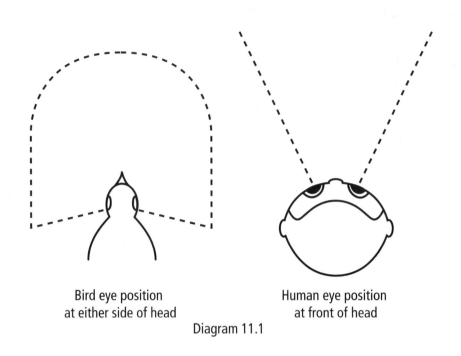

Bird eye position
at either side of head

Human eye position
at front of head

Diagram 11.1

to scan for predators over a wide arc and results in increased sensitivity to movement – a necessity for the survival of hunted animals. Knowing how far the predator is from them is less important than knowing there is one nearby.

Animals that hunt or are tree dwelling like birds of prey, cats or monkeys have their eyes in front of their head. Each eye has a visual field of approximately 170 degrees but the two visual fields overlap to a considerable degree resulting in a much narrower visual field. However, the big advantage of this arrangement is that it gives stereoscopic vision - that is, vision in three dimensions. As a result these animals can judge distances very accurately, a very valuable skill when hunting or jumping from tree to tree. If we accept that man has evolved from tree dwelling animals this explains why human beings have eyes at the front of the head.

How exactly does stereoscopic vision enable us to see in three dimensions and to judge distances?

When we focus on an object in the distance both eyes see almost the same image. However, when we focus on an object close up, each eye will see a slightly different image. It is the fusion of these two slightly different images by the brain, to form a single image, which allows us to view the world in three dimensions and leads to good hand to eye co-ordination.

The angle subtended at the object increases as the object is brought nearer to our eyes (Diagram 11.2) and it is this increase in angle, which enables our brain to work out the distance between the object and our eyes.

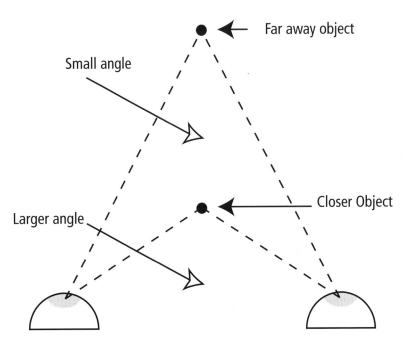

Diagram 11.2   How the eyes judge distance

Demonstration:

Place your index finger vertically at a distance of 30 centimetres (1 foot) at eye level in front of your nose. Focus on an object that is approximately 3 metres (10 feet) behind your finger, say a picture on the wall. Notice that you are able to see two images of your finger, one from each eye. You can check this by closing and opening each eye alternately and noticing how the image of your finger appears to move from side to side.

Holding your index finger in the same place, now focus on your finger as opposed to the picture and you will notice that you can see two images of the picture on the wall.

Each eye works independently of the other in that they each see a separate image. However, they work in tandem to judge distance and enable us to see in three dimensions.

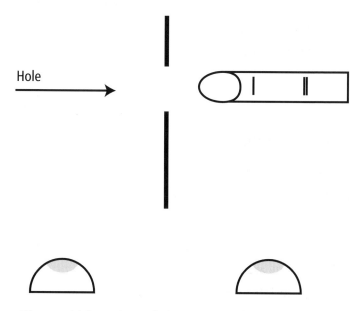

Diagram 11.3   Using Hole in paper to judge distance

Demonstration:

Take a plain piece of paper and cut a hole in the middle about 2.5 cm in diameter. Have somebody hold the paper side-on, such that the edge of the paper is in line with your nose, at a distance of 60 cm (2 feet) away from your face (Diagram11.3). Now simply move your right index finger into the hole in the paper. You will find it quite easy to do this.

Next cover your right-eye with your left hand and ask the other person to move the paper forwards and backwards and stop a distance beyond the 60 cm. Now lean forward and place your right index finger in the hole. Repeat the same procedure covering your left-eye with your left hand and at a different distance again. How accurately did you judge this distance with one eye compared to when you used both eyes?

In order to judge distance accurately, both eyes have to work together and focus on the object that should be in line with the nose. If the object is not in line with the nose the angle subtended at the object will vary and the brain will not be able to compute the distance accurately.

Does the position of the book relative to the eyes make a difference to reading ability?

Some children seem to hold a book to one side of their face whilst others seem to tilt the book so that one side of the book is closer to their face. When reading, most people hold the page of the book directly in front of their eyes such that their nose is in line with the centre of the page. This means that both eyes are roughly the same distance from each word as they scan the page from left to right and that both eyes are therefore focused at the same distance.

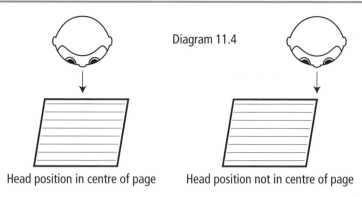

Diagram 11.4

Head position in centre of page   Head position not in centre of page

For a variety of reasons some people hold the page of the book to one side of their face and, if we compare the two diagrams above, it is obvious that when the reader holds their head to one side of the page then both eyes are not then at the same distance from each word. This means that only one eye can be in sharp focus and stereoscopic vision will not be functioning properly. Students who read with a book in this position regularly report that:

(a) The size of the letters changes as they scan across the page.

(b) The letters appear to become "fuzzy" or out of focus on one side of the page.

It is interesting to note that when these students are asked to cover their non-dominant eye and read four or five lines it does not seem to make a difference. However, when they cover their dominant eye and continue to read they find that reading is much more difficult. The dominant eye will be the one in focus and the non-dominant eye will be the one out of focus. *(See Chapter 9 on eye dominance)*.

In the 1950's children often suffered from a "sty" in one eye and the cure was usually an application of ointment and a wad of cotton wool, which was kept in place with an eye patch. It was noted that some children who had reading difficulties in school improved to a degree while wearing the patch. Hence, experiments were carried out on groups of children over a period of time, which showed a strong positive relationship between reading ability and having one eye covered. However, wearing the patch meant the children lost their stereoscopic vision. Their view of the world changed and they were unable to judge distance accurately. This led to children falling down stairs and displaying other clumsy movements, so the practice was abandoned.

Demonstration:

Read the previous paragraph with each eye separately and you will probably find that you read slightly easier with one eye than with the other. Hold the book off centre and repeat the exercise. The difference between reading the paragraph with each eye separately will probably be more obvious. The more off centre the more marked is the difference!

Demonstration:

Read the paragraph again only this time instead of holding the book flat tilt the book so that the left-hand side is closer to you and the book now makes an angle of 45 degrees to the level position. After reading a number of lines you will find that the sharpness, or focus, of the words on the page will vary from one side of the page to the other. You may find that you read the same line twice or indeed skip lines

Conclusion:

Holding a book to the side of the face or tilted at an angle may make a difference to a child's reading ability. They will both affect the functioning of the child's stereoscopic vision because the words will be at different distances from each eye and it will not be possible for both eyes to be in sharp focus at the same time.

N.B. Simply asking the child to hold the book flat or in a central position will not necessarily improve their reading, as this is not their "natural" perceptual head position relative to the book. Specific interventions are necessary to overcome these problems.

Why does my child insist on holding a book "crooked" when reading.

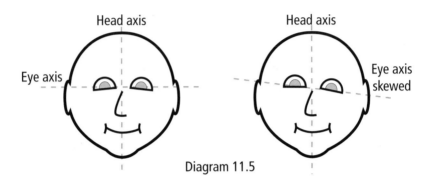

Diagram 11.5

For many people their eye axis (the line running through the centre of the pupils of their eyes) is not horizontal. This can happen for two reasons:-

They may hold their head slightly off vertical when reading. This may result due to the fact that their dominant hand/arm being stronger than the non-dominant hand/arm when holding a book at a very young age and they have retained this reading position in later years.

Even though they hold their head vertical when reading their eye axis may still not be horizontal. The axis of the eyes may not be perpendicular to the head axis. Very few individuals have a perfectly symmetrical face but the lack of symmetry can be quite pronounced for some. If this is the case for your child do not make the child aware of it as this may lead to the child being "self-conscious" of their facial appearance.

Please note that for some students the head axis is slightly off vertical at all times whereas for other students the head axis is normally vertical but only becomes off vertical when reading or examining an object held close to the eyes.

Demonstration:

Read the previous paragraph with the book turned anti-clockwise so that the top edge of the book is held at 45 degrees to the horizontal. How different did this feel? Next turn the book clockwise by the same amount and read the paragraph again. How different did this feel?

For most people the difference will be more marked in one direction than the other depending on their clockwise/anti-clockwise dominance profile. *(See Chapter 10 on clockwise / anti-clockwise dominance)*

Please note

It is important to realise that some people hold a book "crooked" so that the lines of words are in fact parallel to their eye axis. Readers, especially young readers, should therefore be allowed to hold the book as they wish. Instructing a reader to hold the book "straight" when in fact the eye axis, head axis or both are not "straight" greatly inhibits easy reading. A significant number of children prefer to hold the book when reading rather than have the book on a desk or table because of the position of their eye or head axis. It is therefore vitally important that the child is allowed to hold the book in the way that feels "natural".

So how exactly do eyes "see"?

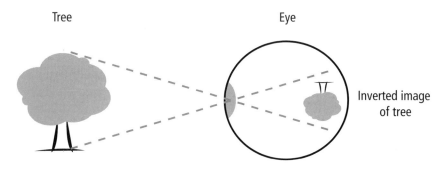

Diagram 11.6

Inverted image on the back of the eye at the retina

According to Diagram 11.6 the eyes see the tree upside down! This is in fact true due to the "inverting" lens at the front of the eye. Experiments have been carried out in which people have worn inverting spectacles containing mirrors that allowed them to perceive everything upside down and back to front. Needless to say, initially the subjects were totally disorientated, had difficulty retaining balance, perceiving the distance objects were away from them and were constantly knocking into things. Yet, after only three or four days, the brain took this "wrong" signal and turned the image the right way up. This emphasises the fact that the brain has the power to interpret, change, distort and modify in many ways the image seen by the eye. Fortunately, after removing the inverting spectacles the brain learned to re-interpret and the subjects were able to see normally again within an even shorter period of time.

If each eye sees a slightly different image how does the brain interpret these so that we are conscious of seeing only one image?

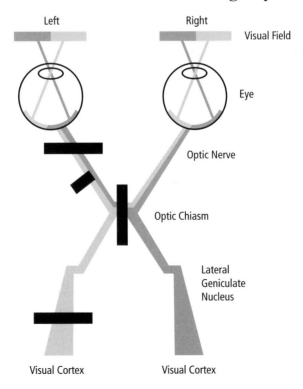

For the purposes of this book, the following is a relatively simplistic view of how our eyes work together to form a single image and how the brain subsequently processes that image.

The visual signals from each eye are merged together in the optic chiasm in a process, which is far more sophisticated than what we can achieve with modern artificial technology.

When we think of a television studio we think of the forefront of technology. Imagine a programme director with two television cameras filming a person being interviewed. One of the cameras is in front of the person giving a full-face view and the other is at the side of the person giving a profile face view.

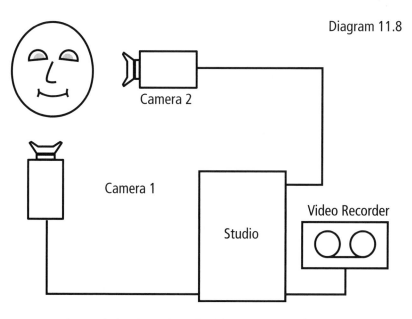

Diagram 11.8

Person being interviewed with TV camera 1 face on
and TV camera 2 to face profile

The programme director can switch between the signals from each camera so that the view received by the audience can alternate between the two views of the face of the person being interviewed. Rather like the programme director our brain receives different signals from each eye but, by contrast, our brain does not accept the signal from one eye or the other but rather combines both signals. The optic chiasm has the ability to take the signal from each eye and, by comparing the difference in colour, contrast and outline of each image, deleting aspects of the image of one eye and emphasising aspects of the image of the other eye, forms a three-dimensional interpretation of the image to transmit to the rest of the brain.

Returning to our programme director, he then feeds the signals he has selected from each camera into a type of large video recorder. The resulting programme can be replayed and transmitted to people in their homes. At any time in the future the programme can be re-transmitted and we see it as a repeat programme on TV. The programme director can also select clips from the programme or several programmes to make a new programme.

Humans have the ability to do something similar. The signals from our eyes are recorded in our brain's visual memory. However, the whole process is much more sophisticated. Not only does our brain combine the signals from each eye, it can manipulate the memories, collect memories together in many different ways and make connections between seemingly unconnected memories.

I think you will agree that our eyes and brain are much, much more complex than even today's modern technology!

As mentioned previously, some people, when reading with one eye, form a sharp image of the words and are able to read as easily as if they were reading with both eyes whereas, when they read with the other eye, the words appear blurred, distorted and "vague". I hope the reader can appreciate now how selective the brain can be with the signal produced in each eye.

In the final stage of the information pathway from the page to the brain, the combined visual signal produced by the optic chiasm is processed in the LGN (Lateral Geniculate Nuclei). Here it is split into its component parts to be delivered to the primary visual cortex, which parcels out information for interpretation by the other specialist visual processing areas. In our programme director analogy, this is equivalent to recording the edited signal on to videotape for programme storage. However, once again the human brain is rather more sophisticated and instead of saving the visual signal in one location, it breaks the signal down into its different component parts such as colour, contrast, outline shape, three dimensional form and other components then each of these is stored separately in our visual memory.

Why does our brain store images in our visual memory in such a complicated fashion?

Consider colour and outline shape, two components of an image stored separately in your visual memory, and imagine a yellow house. The colour of the house will be stored in one part of your visual memory and the outline shape of the house will be stored in another part of your visual memory.

Ask yourself what other objects you know of that are yellow. You may answer a yellow flower, the yellow part of a bee or wasp, the yellow colour of the sun when it is low in the sky, the yellow colour of a particular room you may remember, the yellow markings on the back of a snake you may have seen in the past, the yellow colour you see in traffic lights and so on.

Ask yourself what shapes you see when looking at the house. You may see squares or rectangles when looking at the windows, doors or walls. Now ask yourself what else has the shape of a square or rectangle. A book, a football pitch, a shoebox or the markings of a zebra crossing may come to mind.

So, by considering just two components of an image of a yellow house, we can make connections between the image of the house and many other varied objects. Thus our brain can make numerous and varied "connections" by storing the images of what we see with our eyes as different components in different locations within our visual memory.

This enables us to learn very much more quickly and it also enables us to understand how things work. For example, if we can operate a CD player we can use this knowledge to learn to operate a video recorder much more easily. If we can use a dishwasher we can probably "guess" how to use a washing machine or a tumble dryer. Having learned how to operate one programme on a computer, children are often able to operate any other programme with relative ease. The word processing programme used to produce this book is very similar in user format to database, spreadsheet, diary, or web page programmes. As a result many people find it easy to use a computer because once they have learned how to use one programme they can easily operate several. This ability is greatly enhanced by virtue of the fact that our brain stores the colour and shapes of the keys and icons used by all the programmes separately in different parts of our visual memory.

How do we use the sophisticated memory structure of our brain when learning how to read?

Examine the following letters and decide what shapes are involved.

O   I   L   T   V   X   Z

Now ask yourself where you have seen a shape like the letter O? Some objects might easily spring to mind e.g. a ball, an orange, a clock, a wheel, a CD, the sun. How would you describe the shape of the letter O to a child? What everyday objects would you compare the shape to? How easy would it be for the child to first of all remember the shape and then to make new connections between the shape and the objects you have mentioned? How easy would it be for the child to see and recognise the letter O and also to draw the letter O?

You could also examine the other letters in the list and have a child look for similar shapes in other everyday objects or parts of those objects. An interesting point to consider here is the fact that when we examine a ball or an orange we know that these are three-dimensional objects and yet we can use those to make a connection with the letter O even though it is a two-dimensional letter! Not only does our brain remember the shape of objects but it can also make the connection between the shapes of three-dimensional objects and two-dimensional objects. An explanation of this fact is beyond the realm of this book but it is an interesting fact to consider.

Why are some people more aware of shape or colour than others?

As we have already discussed the two images produced by our eyes are combined into a single image that is then separated into its component parts, which in turn are stored separately in various different memory locations. However, our brains can go a step further and consciously select which component of the image is more important to us – that may be shape, colour or any other component – although our selection may quite often be dictated more by parental and cultural influences than by free choice ......in itself an interesting thought!!

It is generally agreed that females are more colour conscious than males. Women in general are more conscious about the colour co-ordination of their clothes and the interior decoration of a house than men. Men in general are more concerned about outline shape. According to the automobile industry men are much more conscious about the shape of a car than women are. Perhaps this is why there are more men than women who are architects and more women than men who are interior designers. It seems that the culture of men and women who live in the Western world tends to result in women placing more emphasis on colour and men placing more emphasis on shape.

Why do some children learn their letters easily and others find it more difficult?

It would seem from the above discussion that some people (not necessarily males!) place more emphasis on shape whereas others place more emphasis on colour. It would be easier to teach a child letters by using the shapes of letters if that child were "shape conscious". However, if a child is not "shape conscious", learning letters will not be so easy and there are two possible reasons why this could be the case. Firstly, the child may not be aware of the shapes of everyday objects. A child brought up in a flat barren environment will not be as "regular shape" conscious as a child brought up in a more man-made environment. It would seem reasonable then that the child from the flat barren desert environment would find it more difficult to learn the shapes of letters. Secondly, the child may not be able to make a connection between a three-dimensional object and a two-dimensional shape. Children brought up in a rain forest environment, when first introduced to drawing on paper, can have severe difficulty in relating a two-dimensional image to their normal three-dimensional world.

How can I encourage my child to become more shape conscious and more easily recognise letters?

As discussed above, we can consciously pay attention to particular components of an image and shape is no exception.

When we look at the drawings of pre-school children we have to use a great degree of imagination and interpretation to appreciate these fine works of art! This is because the child's ability to interpret the shapes he sees is not fully developed and neither is his hand to eye co-ordination, which depends on the brain being able to interpret shape. We can only draw a picture when we have the image in our head.

By cutting out pieces of cardboard in different shapes, e.g. a square, a circle, a triangle and a rectangle, a child can be encouraged to explore different shapes and begin to understand concepts such as vertical and horizontal straight lines, curves, right angles etc. Each of the shapes should have a different colour and perhaps a different surface. We can use sand paper, shiny paper, corrugated cardboard, tinfoil, cling film so that the child will not only see the different shapes but also feel the different shapes.

Once the child is able to identify two or three of the shapes then they can hold the shape up against everyday objects, for example, the television, a door, a ball, and a table leg, to compare and find the shape of these everyday objects. Next the child should be encouraged to see different shapes in everyday objects e.g. examine a car to see the circles of the wheels and the steering wheel and the speedometer, find a square shape in the windows and doors, find the triangle of the quarter light windows, find a straight edge across the boot door, find a right angle on the seat.

As a child becomes more "shape conscious" then he/she can be introduced to large letters cut out from pieces of cardboard. Examine the circle of an O, look at the right angles of an L and a T and notice the difference between them, examine the straight edge of an I. Once the child becomes aware of shape the next step of letter recognition becomes much easier.

Pre-school experience has an enormous influence on how a child "sees" the world. All children should be introduced to multi-sensory perception. The use of colour, shape and texture etc. should be encouraged. When a baby is born it is highly touch-sensitive for feeding and cuddling. This is followed by the development of sight as they begin to recognise faces and shapes and subsequently they begin to associate those feelings and images with sounds. It seems only natural then that we use the same sequence to teach letters.

It may be interesting to read the following as it may help us appreciate how complicated our sense of vision is in relation to our recognition of letters, words and sentences.

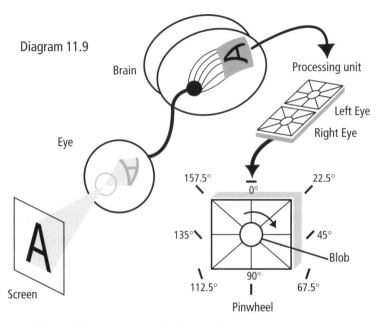

Scheme of the eye seeing the letter A showing cortical processing
and pinwheel arrangement of neurons that respond to line orientation

Let us examine how we see the letter A. The letter A appears upside down on the back of the eye (the retina), which acts like a film at the rear of a camera. The photoreceptor cells on the surface of the retina detect the light and send an electrical signal along the nerve fibres, via the optic chiasm, to the Lateral Geniculate Nuclei (LGN). The signals from both the left-eye and righ-eye are combined and interpreted as a single signal. This interpreted signal then passes from the LGN, as its component parts, to various parts of the visual cortex that lies at the back of the brain. Hence the letter A is encoded as three separate lines (/ - \) by the LGN and each line is stored separately in the visual cortex. In other words each letter of the alphabet is not encoded in the visual memory of the brain as a complete letter but as each of its constituent parts.

Let us examine the word better:

better

The letter b has two constituent parts, each letter e has three constituent parts, each t has three constituent parts and the r has two constituent parts. So, even in a simple six-letter word such as "better", there are a total of 16 constituent parts, each of which is stored in a different part of the visual cortex. To read this word we have to de-code each constituent part of each letter by comparing each part to that constituent part which we have stored in our visual cortex. By doing this with each of the 16 parts and adding these memories together we are able to remember the visual representation of the word "better" as a whole and only then do we cross over to our auditory memory to remember the sound of the word. A break in any single link of this chain will result in difficulty reading the word "better"? Remember also that "better" is a relatively simple word because it contains two e's and two t's!

What has been outlined in this chapter is only a very brief summary of how we actually see words and letters but it is hoped that this explanation will give you some appreciation of the difficulty some individuals have when reading individual words and sentences. You will now understand why some people can recognise certain letters but not others i.e. the brain has a visual memory of some of the constituent components of letters but not others. The importance of finding which particular link in the chain is missing is vital so that relevant help can be offered to these individuals.

Chapter 12

Visual dyslexia

Visual and physical symptoms associated with light sensitivity

Some students with dyslexia claim that the words move on the page or words move into each other, or letters and words sometimes become fuzzy or other such phenomena as result of their sensitivity to light. This only affects a minority of students who have reading difficulties and is not to be confused with the earlier chapter that dealt with visual effects due to eye-tracking difficulties. The phenomena dealt with in this chapter are due to external factors such as the lighting in a room where the student is reading, rather than eye-tracking difficulties (Chapter 5).

Why do some students complain that words move on a page or that they see blotches, diamonds or circles on a page when they are reading?

Why do some students complain of "tired eyes" (Asthenopia) or a "sore head" when they read?

Why do some students complain they are physically uncomfortable when reading?

If words appear to move on a page or the student sees blotches, diamonds or circles which are not there, it is easy to understand how the student finds reading tiring and avoids reading whenever possible. As a result, reading is not practised and therefore does not improve and this in turn creates frustration for the parent. If the parent forces the student to read, the student expresses discomfort and the parent feels sympathy but then feels frustration because the child is not practising reading ………….. and so the cycle continues!

Frequently a parent or a teacher will notice that a student's eyes feel uncomfortable when reading and the student will be taken to an optician. The student will have a standard eye examination which tests for long or short sightedness, astigmatism and other such refractive problems. The optician will also check for signs of disease in the eye, a pathological examination. More often than not, the student is given the "all clear" but still the parent and the teacher suspect there is "something wrong with how the student sees".

In a severe case the student may even complain of having a headache or discomfort associated with either one or both eyes.

One possible cause of the problems is that the student has eye-tracking difficulties, which have already been discussed in Chapter 5. Another possible cause is that the student is susceptible to glare or light sensitivity or other physical factors.

Glare (Light sensitivity, Photophopia)

Some individuals, whether or not they have reading problems, complain of glare, which is due to the contrast of black letters on a white background that is accentuated by bright light.

Which of the following text boxes is easier for you to read?

1. Which of these text boxes is easier for you to read?

2. Which of these text boxes is easier for you to read?

If you chose 2 then it is likely you wear sunglasses in the summer and prefer to read in the shade rather than having sunlight falling directly on the page. You are susceptible to glare to some degree.

Demonstration:

Look at a bright light e.g. a desk lamp for ten seconds, then look through a set of open Venetian blinds for five seconds and then immediately look at the ceiling above. You will notice that your eyes perceive the pattern of the Venetian blinds on the ceiling as a series of alternate dark and bright lines. The edges of these lines will not be sharp but will appear fuzzy.

The degree to which a person experiences the above will vary from individual to individual.

In northern Europe, where the number of days with blue skies and bright sunshine are rare, people are unaccustomed to the bright light and a high degree of colour and contrast. On a bright sunny day some people will find the light too intense and wear sunglasses but some will not and this is due to the fact that some individuals are more susceptible to glare than others.

Certain people find it difficult to read outside on a very sunny day or even beside a window through which the sun is shining and this is due to a low tolerance of glare. This can be reduced either by wearing tinted glasses, or more simply by covering the page with a sheet of tinted transparent plastic. The colour of the tint may vary from light pink, through green and yellow, to light blue. Many people choose blue or mauve tints to alleviate their particular difficulty with glare but again that will vary from individual to individual.

Demonstration:

Place a book on a flat surface and shine a desk lamp onto the page, at a distance of two feet (60 cm), and read one page. Next move the desk lamp until it is only six inches (15 cm) from the page and read the page. If the light is bright enough you will experience glare when you are reading. Next take a hi-lighter and use it to highlight about 10 lines of text. Again, with the lamp at a distance of six inches (15 cm) read the ten lines and you will become aware of the difference in the glare. The effect of the glare will be different, depending whether you use a yellow, pink, green or blue hi-lighter, and it will be different for each individual.

Pattern glare

The effects of ordinary glare as demonstrated above are well known and easy to understand. However, there is a related phenomenon, known as pattern glare, which is less well known and is induced by small simple repeating patterns.

Demonstration:

Do not try out this demonstration if you suffer from, or suspect you suffer from, migraine or epilepsy!

Look at the low-grade pattern glare chart on the following page and focus on the centre of the pattern for short period of time. You may well experience pattern glare and "see" visual hallucinations in the form of blotches, vibration, movement, patches, diamonds, or loss of edge sharpness. The experience will be different for each individual. Do not look at the chart for too long as it may well induce an unpleasant feeling.

Demonstration:

Another illustration of pattern glare! Look at the squares below and count the dots.

Of course there are no dots but they seem to be there and to be switching on and off. This optical illusion is caused by pattern glare.

Pattern glare is dependent upon several variables:

1. The colour of the text and the colour of the page.

2. The degree of contrast between the colour of the text and the colour of the page.

3. The spacing between the lines of text.

4. The type of light being used to read, either fluorescent or normal bulbs.

5. Whether you hold the pattern straight in front or at an angle of 30 degrees or more. (The effect of this is to reduce the amount of pattern glare.)

For some people, reading the printed word in a normal book can also induce pattern glare induced as above. Imagine when you look at words on the page they seem similar to the black boxes above and hence black spots or blotches switch on and off between the words. Can you imagine how uncomfortable it would be to read while experiencing pattern glare?

Pattern glare can be greatly reduced by using books with larger print and greater spacing between the lines. Students suffering from pattern glare will sometimes tilt their book at an angle to their mid-line, either clockwise or anti-clockwise. This reduces pattern glare but definitely does not help the normal eye-tracking movements, and often results in the student skipping lines or reading the same line again. The parent or teacher may well ask the student to hold the book straight, not realising that this induces pattern glare for the student!

Demonstration:

Look at the lines below, are they parallel?

They do not appear to be parallel but if you turn the book clockwise through 45 degrees, the lines will now look parallel. In the same way, some students when reading will hold a book at varying angles from 15 to 45 degrees to the vertical, in order to make the lines look parallel rather than "bendy".

What are the signs of visual problems?

Please note: No individual would exhibit all these symptoms, but if they exhibit several then it may indicate a specific visual problem, which, may or may not affect reading.

Encountering problems with sunshine (squinting/rubbing of the eyes)

Complaining of having "sore eyes"

Having headaches in front of the head/above the eyes

Having a "lazy eye"

Trying to reduce the light level in a room

Developing red eyes when reading

Apparent swelling in the eye area while reading (can be often be misdiagnosed as allergies)

Rubbing eyes when reading

Blinking more often when reading

Covering one eye when reading (Voluntary Occlusion)

Skipping words when reading

Have concentration problems

Migraine headaches

Avoiding reading

Recommendations:

It is essential that students who suffer from glare or pattern glare do not read beside a window in the classroom or place of study, with direct sunlight falling upon the page.

Some people have reported coloured lenses helpful when reading. However an inexpensive solution to is to purchase coloured overlay sheets at a stationery shop and place them over the page to be read. Vary the colours over a period of time. Parents should be aware that a child may enjoy the novelty of this in the short term and "perceive a difference" but the improvement may wear off. The reason the effect may wear off is that if we wear sunglasses for a period, then we start to perceive colour as well as if we did not wear the sunglasses. The human brain may receive a signal from the eye but it can learn to manipulate that signal!

The students should refrain from reading under a fluorescent light as reading with a normal incandescent bulb can greatly reduce pattern glare. This is due to the fact that fluorescent tubes flicker, even though it is not perceptible under normal circumstances.

For these students holding the book at a slight angle of rotation can also reduce pattern glare and they should be allowed to hold the book as they wish.

Students who are light sensitive may also benefit from using coloured paper when writing.

Individuals who regularly use computers may wish to change the background colour and/or adjust the brightness/contrast on the monitor, rather than the normal white background.

Research for a purely visual cause of dyslexia has been carried out over a considerable period of time with various spectacles and apparatus. As yet there is no firm empirical independent evidence as to the benefits of these aids. However, in the media, headlines indicating that such devices provide a 'cure' are commonplace.

Many studies have been carried out on the physical eye movements of people when they are reading. Such studies have been carried out on people with and without dyslexia and the results compared. There do seem to be measurable differences both in the speed and pattern of eye-tracking although, at the time of writing, such differences appear to be an aspect of dyslexia rather than a cause of it.

Remember we do not all "see" the world the same way, and perception varies but there is no right and wrong, just different!

Some terms which an ophthalmic optician or an optometrist may use:

Asthenopia:

Screwing of the eyes, squinting of both eyes, aggravation of the eyes or other eye discomfort that is not due to disease.

Accommodation Anomalies:

The ability of the eyes to focus on objects close to the distance of the "least distance of distinct vision". Students copying down words from the black /white board sometimes complain that words appear to be "fuzzy".

Convergence Insufficiency:

The eyes are unable to turn in independently whilst viewing an object approaching the bridge of the nose from a distance.

Fusional Reserve Reduction:

Each eye sees one image and it is important that both images converge otherwise two images that do not exactly overlap produce what some students term "double vision".

Photophobia

Lack of tolerance of bright light situations leading to excessive watering of the eyes, squinting or screwing up of the eyes.

Saccadal Eye Movement Problems:

When reading the eyes do not move in a smooth fashion across a line of words, instead they move in small distinct movements. This discontinuous movement is caused as the eyes fall on a word. They must both, first of all, converge on the word, and then subsequently they must both focus on the word by using small movements of both eyes. There have been many studies on the eye movement of readers with dyslexia e.g. Newman 1989, Evans 1993, Pavlidis1981, Rayner 1983, Fischer and Biscaldi 1994.

Chapter 13

Suggestions to help students who have dyslexia in a classroom environment

I have taught in schools in Ireland for 23 years and have listened to "advice from experts" many times during those years. Whilst some of the advice was useful and theoretically beneficial, putting it into practice would have been extremely time-consuming and, although it may have worked with small groups or with an individual student, it would not have worked in a normal class environment with groups of students of 20 or more. The following advice has been tried and tested in an everyday classroom environment.

Location of the student in the classroom:

Most people, when attending a lecture or presentation and can choose freely where they sit, will usually sit in a preferred location. Some people like to sit at the back, others to one side, others in the middle, and others at the front etc. - this does not happen just by chance. For example, if one has a dominant right ear and likes to listen to a lecture in detail one would probably like to sit on the left-hand side of a room as this allows the dominant right ear to listen intently. Other people may like to write a lot of notes when listening to a lecture and therefore will need a good source of light so that they can clearly see what they are writing. Some people like to sit at the front of a lecture theatre so that they can see the facial expressions of the lecturer and be close to the screen or the black/white board. Other people like to sit at the back of a room so that they can preserve their anonymity and so avoid being asked to give any feedback whatsoever.

People make a choice where they sit for many reasons other than those suggested above but, by and large, people do choose where they sit. I have been asked at times by students if they may switch position in the classroom and, like most teachers, immediately questioned why. There are of course times when a teacher may suspect that they want to talk to their best friend, or be less attentive at the back of the classroom, or perhaps view an attractive looking classmate from a closer distance. However, where a student sits in a classroom can be of significant importance to that student and this can be particularly so for a student with dyslexia.

The location of the window or windows in a classroom affects not only the amount of light that comes into a classroom but also the degree of direct sunlight. Some students with dyslexia who also have eye-tracking problems may be affected by glare *(see Chapter 12)*. In the British Isles we do not seem to have many days of sunshine and it is interesting to see how many people reach for their sunglasses when the sun does come out because they are not "used to the sun". Other people are delighted at the sight of the sun and would not think of wearing sunglasses. It seems that glare does not affect everybody in the same way.

As referred to earlier, some people with dyslexia tend to "focus" on the white page rather than on the black print and hence, if direct sunlight falls on the page, they are more likely to be affected by the sunlight. A student who is affected by glare and feels distinctly uncomfortable when seated at a window in direct sunshine should be allowed to sit in a shaded part of the classroom.

Some students with dyslexia who perceive the white page more than the black print are often susceptible to shadows on the page. If such a student is reading and the light is behind his head, the shadow of his head will appear on the page and this will often be a source of distraction to such a student. To eradicate this problem such students should sit with the overhead light in front of them.

A lot of students complain of the "shine" on the blackboard whereas others do not. Simply moving the student sideways in the classroom solves the problem of reflected light from the black/white board.

What is not so obvious is that some students have an optimum distance from the blackboard. Students with dyslexia should be encouraged to sit at different distances from the blackboard and to copy down a list of words. The accuracy and the speed with which they copy down words can vary enormously as the distance increases or decreases and can be different for each individual student with dyslexia. There does not seem to be a general correlation between accuracy of copying and a particular distance from the blackboard but for a significant number of students with dyslexia, the distance from the blackboard makes a significant difference and the distance is variable from pupil to pupil.

As mentioned before a student's dominant ear has a major bearing on which side of the classroom he/she prefers to sit. It is easy to test which ear is dominant.

Demonstration:

Pretend two people are talking on the other side of a wall. Walk up to the wall and put your ear to the wall to listen to the conversation. Whichever ear you use is your dominant ear. Step back a few steps then approach the wall and put the other ear to the wall. Notice how different it feels to try to listen with the ear that is not dominant.

Demonstration:

Try watching the television from one side of a room for ten or fifteen minutes and then continue to watch from the other side of a room for a period of time. For a significant number of people this makes a difference. If it makes a difference when watching television then it will certainly make a difference when watching or listening to a teacher in a classroom environment.

If you were reading this as a teacher you would be forgiven for asking "How am I going to test the students in the class for each of the above and then work out where each student should sit in the classroom?" It is not necessary to do this, as each student will know his own "preference". It is only important to realise that the student's preferred location has a physical reason and is not just a "notion".

Visual presentation of course work

Students with dyslexia find it difficult, if not impossible, to listen and take down efficient and usable notes at the same time. The importance of a teacher summarising a lesson on the blackboard cannot be overestimated.

Such students have great difficulty copying down written work at the same speed as students who do not have dyslexia. As we all know it is not essential to make full sentences, paragraphs or even essays to yield a set of notes that can be used to put a subject in perspective or as an aid for revision. The following are some suggestions to enable a student to minimise the amount of note taking whilst at the same time providing aid for revision and an opportunity for holistic learning.

Textbooks:

When I was a student textbooks consisted mainly of written words and they were very expensive items compared to my parents' annual salary. Nowadays, school textbooks are much more appealing and relatively much less expensive.

Modern textbooks have many diagrams, pictures, charts and tables and use colour. In the past, with traditional typesetting methods, the cost of colour and diagrams was prohibitive but today, with computers and modern printing methods, the cost of using colour and diagrams in textbooks has been reduced significantly.

Modern textbooks are generally paperback rather than hardback. When textbooks were hardback we were instructed to take great care of them by both parents and teachers, as they were often handed down from one generation of students to another and to brothers and sisters. Nowadays, courses change so much and so often that textbooks are paperback and replaced much more frequently. I mention this as the following advice flies in the face of what is generally accepted, particularly by older generations.

Students with dyslexia should be encouraged to write on their textbooks!

When a student with dyslexia is asked to revise from a textbook it is a very time-consuming exercise and anything that reduces this time is a huge advantage.

Using highlighters to mark out those parts of the text, which are essential, very important or important immediately reduces the time for revision. The student should be encouraged to devise a colour code system e.g. yellow for headings and summaries, blue for definitions and laws and perhaps green for useful quotes, phrases, dates or statistics.

Key words or phrases written in the margins or at the top or bottom of the page can be very helpful for revising work covered in class. A key word with an arrow pointing to one or two relevant places on the page will greatly help the student when trying to summarise the text.

A keyword with the numbers of all the other relevant pages in the book may serve to bring together various strands of a particular concept from different parts of the book.

As stated before, the use of diagrams in modern textbooks has made them much more attractive for students to use. It should not be forgotten that a diagram, no matter how simple, drawn by a student himself is even more useful as it is his personal overview of what he understands to be the concept behind the text. Students with dyslexia should be encouraged to draw such diagrams and the most relevant place to put these diagrams is in the book whether in the margins of the book, in the blank spaces provided at the end of chapters, or even on a piece of paper attached with sticky tape or stapled onto a page.

Remember the old adage "A picture is worth more than a thousand words"? This is even more relevant for a student with dyslexia as it is much quicker to read a picture than it is to read a thousand words! The topic of mind maps will be dealt with later in this chapter.

Black/white board presentation

As referred to in Chapter 5 under the topic of eye-tracking difficulties, some students with dyslexia may find it difficult to copy from the black/white board. These difficulties can be minimised simply and with little effort as follows.

Divide the board vertically into three segments (left, middle and right) and horizontally into two segments (top and bottom). This immediately reduces the difficulty for a student with dyslexia – "Where am I on the board?" – and yet it only takes a second or two for these lines to be drawn. It is so easy for a student with dyslexia to lose their place when copying down a sentence from the board when it is written along the full width of the board.

Lists of words appear on the blackboard regularly. These lists can consist of a list of spellings, a verb in a foreign language, a list of apparatus for an experiment etc. When writing out these lists some students can get confused (See vertical confusion in Chapter 5). Simply writing a number or letter beside each word can easily alleviate the confusion. This will not make much difference to a student without dyslexia but will make a huge difference to a student with dyslexia.

For example:

Camel

Elephant

Tiger

Hippopotamus

Alligator

Rhinoceros

If a student with dyslexia is asked to copy down such a list from the black/white board into an exercise book he/she may have some difficulty. He/she will copy down the first word, then the second word and perhaps even the third word. However, when he/she comes to the fourth word confusion arises and he/she loses where he/she is on the board. The normal solution is for the student to look at the exercise book to find the word they have taken down last and look for that word on the blackboard to find "where they are on the black/white board". This is time consuming and can leave a student with dyslexia feeling under considerable time pressure in the classroom.

The solution to the above is:

1. Camel	*or*	**a.** Camel
2. Elephant		**b.** Elephant
3. Tiger		**c.** Tiger
4. Hippopotamus		**d.** Hippopotamus
5. Alligator		**e.** Alligator
6. Rhinoceros		**f.** Rhinoceros

It is easy for the student with dyslexia to follow the order as a series of numbers or letters.

Use coloured chalk or markers to highlight headings, definitions, laws, verbs, formula, dates and other important facts. When the teacher uses a colour code system on the board and is seen to adhere to it, the students will follow. It is amazing to examine the exercise books of a younger student at second level and see the variation in the style of note taking. This variation reflects the fact that teachers present their notes in different ways on the board and the student follows the same system. If the teacher is systematic with the use of colour, underlining and outlined boxes then the student will adopt the same systematic method thus increasing his/her level of learning and the speed at which he/she learns.

As a teacher please remember that the student with dyslexia will take longer to copy work down from the black/white board and that anything the teacher can do to facilitate this process will increase the speed of note taking by the student with dyslexia. Anything that makes the class run more smoothly and quickly is also beneficial to the teacher!

Handouts

To prepare a handout for a class in the traditional way takes considerable time, effort and patience for the teacher. However, the advent of new technology means that well presented handouts can now be produced much more easily. It is relatively easy to use a computer scanner to scan in text or information from leaflets, posters or other books with the publisher's permission. Once scanned into the computer the text can be manipulated very easily. Some students with dyslexia find it difficult to read small print. Reading books in primary school usually have large print and extra space between the lines to facilitate reading for younger children, as they do not yet have efficient eye-tracking skills. Some older children and adults with dyslexia still do not have efficient eye-tracking skills. Consequently, this book has been written with larger print and a greater space between the lines to make it easier to read for people who do not have efficient eye-tracking skills.

When manipulating text on a computer, chapters can be highlighted and the font size changed at the click of a button. It is so much easier for someone with an eye-tracking problem to read font size 12 rather than font size 8.

Demonstration:

When you read this sentence it is written in font size 12.

When you read this sentence you are reading it with a font size of 8.

The difference in ease of reading different font size is sizeable!

Line spacing is very important when preparing material for a student with dyslexia to read. This paragraph of the book is written with single line spacing (1.0) whereas the rest of the book is written with one and a half line spacing (1.5). The normal reader will find it much easier to read a book with 1.5 line spacing but the reason the publishers normally publish a book with single line spacing and font size 10, as this paragraph, is because it is cheaper to produce as the book uses less paper. For most people who do not have an eye-tracking problem this does not make much difference. However, for the student with dyslexia it makes a huge difference. Furthermore, it is good practice to write notes with one and a half or even double line spacing as it provides space for the student to write in his own notes and relevant thoughts. As teachers we are all keen to encourage students to think for themselves and writing their own notes on top of a handout can be very good practice indeed.

Demonstration:

Read the same paragraph again below (font size 12 and double spacing) and you may even write your own notes between the lines. Imagine what it would be like to write your notes on top of paragraph above, it could well turn out to be a complete mess!

Line spacing is very important when preparing material for a student with dyslexia to read. This paragraph of the book is written with double line spacing (2.0) whereas the rest of the book is written with one and a half line spacing (1.5). The normal reader will find it much easier to read a book with 1.5 line spacing but the reason the publishers normally publish a book with single line spacing and font size 10 is because it is cheaper to produce as the book uses less paper. For most people who do not have an eye-tracking problem this does not make much difference. However, for the student with dyslexia it makes a huge difference. Furthermore, it is good practice to write notes with one and a half or even double line spacing as it provides space for the student to write in his own notes and relevant thoughts. As teachers we are all keen to encourage students to think for themselves and writing their own notes on top of a handout can be very good practice indeed.

Notes that are meant to be a summary of a lesson, text or an essay should not be long winded but be precise, to the point and laid out in such a way that they can be easily revised. The use of the bullet points on the computer has a dramatic effect on revision notes for students who have dyslexia. Reproduced below is a summary of the chapter so far but given as a series of bulleted headings. Read over these bulleted headings again and you will find you can very quickly revise the content of the chapter so far.

Demonstration:

Read the bulleted summary below.

Location of student in the classroom

• Side of the classroom (ear dominance)

• Distance from the blackboard/white board

• Location of window

Visual presentation of course work

(Students with dyslexia have difficulty coping with visual information and instructions, which is why visual presentation of course work is so important.)

Textbooks

• Write on the textbook!

• Use different coloured highlighters

• Key words written in margins

• Diagrams

Blackboard/white board presentation

• Divide the board vertically into three or four segments and horizontally into two segments

• Use chalk/markers of different colours

• Use underlining/box headings

• A student with dyslexia will take longer to copy work down from the black/white board

Handouts:

• Use computer to scan text and other information

• Font size 12/14

• Line spacing double

• Bullet points

For a teacher computers can save an enormous amount of time and effort and it only takes a comparatively short time to learn to use a computer effectively. If you don't know how to use a computer, scanner etc. ask one of your colleagues who does rather than go to a general computer instruction course. Your colleague will know how a computer is useful in the classroom, will cut out unnecessary stuff you do not need and, as a colleague, will know how to teach not to mention reduce costs!

After reading this summary you will appreciate how much easier this format will be for revision purposes for a student with dyslexia, cutting down overall reading time and making it so much easier to read and retain information to be learned.

Mind maps or spider diagrams

The use of mind maps or spider diagrams has been encouraged by Tony Buzan and others for the last thirty or forty years for all students. The potential benefit to students with dyslexia is enormous as it cuts down on the amount of reading, verbal memory work and time taken for revision. Students with dyslexia enjoy using colour and symbols and rapidly acquire the skills necessary to prepare and use mind maps effectively for revision.

Reading material for students with dyslexia

Please refer to Chapter 14 – Suitable reading material for students with dyslexia.

Song lyrics

Most students at school enjoy singing songs. They especially enjoy singing pop songs. It is very easy to obtain the lyrics of all modern pop songs on the Internet. Refer to the Chapter 14 on reading material for students with dyslexia, which deals with obtaining information from the Internet. Use a search engine to look up "name of pop singer or group + lyrics" or perhaps look up "title of song + lyrics". (Do not forget to leave a space either side of the + sign.)

It is a straightforward exercise to obtain the lyrics of a pop song, transfer it into a Word document on a computer and print off a copy for each student in the classroom. Please ensure that the font size is about 14 and that there is double line spacing. First of all play the music in the classroom and allow the students to follow the written words. Make sure each child can recognise each word of the song sheet. Next allow the class as a group to sing along with the music. Encourage the children to sing along at home with the music.

This exercise encourages several skills. It develops word recognition skills, it increases the speed with which the children read, it enables you to point out how words "rhyme" in songs and of course it also develops singing skills.

If the student has suitable computer skills then of course they can find the lyrics of the type of "music" which they enjoy on the Internet themselves.

My hero

Most students at school identify with a hero either on the sports field, in the world of music, world of fashion etc. It is more than useful to encourage the student to look up information on the Internet about their particular hero. Encourage the student to "copy and paste" into a Word document leaving large empty spaces where they should be encouraged to write in their own information on their hero.

A useful exercise for children with dyslexia is to select one of the famous people with learning differences, *(See Chapter 19)* who they admire or identify with. It is interesting to repeat the "My Hero" exercise with several of these famous people. It is more than interesting to find out why they identify with their chosen famous person. By encouraging the student to discuss the project the teacher can get a wonderful insight into how the student "views the world".

Chapter 14

Suitable reading material for students with dyslexia

What is suitable material for students with dyslexia to read?

I am often asked by parents and teachers what I think is suitable reading material for a student who has dyslexia. To expect a student with dyslexia who is trying to improve reading skills to pick up a book that is of minimal interest to him/her and read it from cover to cover is like asking a child who has just learned to ride a bicycle to cycle around the world with two flat tyres and twisted handlebars! Reading material should always be of "interest" to the person reading whether or not they have dyslexia. At school, students have a fixed curriculum to follow and inevitably have prescribed textbooks to read. However, when I deal with a student with dyslexia my goal for success is always the same.

A student should read because he/she wants to read!!!

When I read a Sunday newspaper I read the following sections: current affairs, book review, classical music review, film review, the motoring section and the sports section. I read these sections because they are the areas of interest to me! I do not read the travel section, the fashion section, the business section, suggestions for recipes or the food and drink section because they do not interest me.

Read the following paragraph and ask yourself at the end whether you found it interesting and fascinating?

Dinosaurs evolved from other reptiles during the Triassic period that began approximately 248 million years ago. During this period the biggest mass extinction known occurred on Earth, which was known as The Permian extinction. Extinction results when evolution causes the death rate to increase dramatically over the birth rate, and the species die out. The Archosaurs were groups of reptiles that dominated the earth prior to the

Triassic period, from which the dinosaurs evolved. This group include the Crocodilians, Pterosaurs, Thecodonts, Dinosaurs and Birds. The Thecodonts, which are Crocodile-like Archosuars may have been the direct ancestors of the dinosaurs. The first dinosaurs were approximately 3 – 4.5meters long. Small and lightly built, they were quite agile and fast and were supposedly bipedal carnivores or omnivores.

When you read this paragraph was the internal voice inside your head animated, excited or enthusiastic? Did you make detailed, vivid pictures in your mind? Did you want to read more on the subject? If your answer is "no" to any of these questions then you are not interested in this topic and you will not have enjoyed the reading material! So how would you feel if you were asked to read a complete book on the subject of dinosaurs or, even worse, were asked to read a series of books on the subject! Everyone is an individual and has individual tastes and, as far as reading material is concerned, those individual tastes should be met!

If your son is interested in football then he should read material relating to football. If he is interested in a particular football club, then he should read material relating to that particular football club. If he is interested in a particular football player, then he should read material pertaining to that particular football player.

The first rule for reading material is that it must be of interest!

There are many bookshops, each with many books on the shelves. Many of the books are wonderfully well illustrated, the layout is perfect, the use of colour is magnificent and they can be expensive. Parents often buy expensive books for their children, which are scarcely looked at let alone read with enthusiasm. This may be because the book is out of date. Nowadays, a book six months old may be out of date. The pop group may be out of the charts, the particular football player may have been sold to another team, the particular type of clothes may be considered past it etc. We live in a modern changing world where tastes of what is acceptable or "in" and what is unacceptable or "out" change yearly, monthly, weekly or even daily!

The Internet is a wonderful development for children, students and adults with dyslexia. It provides an endless supply of articles that are up to the minute and beautifully illustrated with pictures and diagrams to stimulate anyone's interest! It is there at a touch of a button, it is available 24 hours a day, it is available seven days a week, it is available in almost every library, it is available in schools, it is available in an ever increasing number of homes and it is very inexpensive, only the price of a phone call away!

The second rule for reading material is that the reading material should be well illustrated, up-to-date and as reasonably priced as possible. The most up-to-date, well-illustrated and best value for money material is on the "THE INTERNET" and it is virtually FREE!

How do I use the Internet to find suitable material for my son or daughter?

This book is not intended to be sexist in any way but let us suppose we have a boy who is interested in football, his favourite team is Manchester United and his favourite player is David Beckham or a boy who loves Lord of the Rings. We also have a girl who is interested in pop music, her favourite group is Westlife and her favourite singer is Robbie Williams or a girl who has a favourite Disney character. All you have to do is to go to the computer, log on to a search engine, click a button and an almost endless supply of links and written material can be downloaded onto the screen, copied and pasted into a Word document and printed out.

I don't know anything about the Internet or computers so how do I get all this free, interesting and useful material?

The following instructions are written so that they can be followed as easily as possible. However, if you are still unsure what to do, visit your local library or go to a computer shop or retailer and ask for a demonstration using the instructions below. Perhaps the most humiliating experience is to ask a teenager for a demonstration but this can be the easiest way to learn, and perhaps you might feel what it is like to have a "learning difficulty"!!!!!!!

The main thing to remember is that a computer cannot explode or burst into flames no matter what button you press!! As far as a computer is concerned, you cannot do anything wrong provided you do not touch the DEL (delete) button!!

Once you have logged on to the Internet, use one of the most popular search engines:

Google – general and popular search engine.

Yahoo! – provider of comprehensive online products and services to consumers and businesses worldwide.

Excite – provides search, news, email, personals, portfolio tracking, and other services.

Lycos – develops and provides online guides to locate and filter information on the Internet. Products enable users to accurately identify and select information of interest to them.

Netscape Search – combines results from the Internet, Open Directory and the Web.

AltaVista – portal featuring web and newsgroup search engine as well as paid submission services.

HotBot – offers users a point-and-click interface, pull down menus, and the ability to use plain English terminology for constructing searches.

AOL Search – search engine and directory.

After you have "logged on" to the search engine just type a key word into the box and click the search button. If you have typed in the name of a famous person you will be greeted with perhaps hundreds of "links". Just click on "blue print" and you will be given more information than you thought possible. Select the written material you want, by highlighting it with the mouse and click on "Edit" and "Copy" it.

Next open your Word programme and select a "New Blank Document" by clicking on the icon. Click on the "Edit" button and select "Paste" and the material you have selected from the web site will be copied into the Word document.

Highlight all of the text by dragging the mouse and then click on "Format" followed by "Font" and change the "Font Size" to 14. Next click on "Format" followed by "Paragraph" followed by "Line Spacing" and select "Double Spacing". You can even highlight all of the text and select "Bold" for the entire document.

Now simply print the reading material out using the printer. The student can write notes on it, draw diagrams on it or whatever, as the original can be kept on file using the computer! This is a wonderful advantage for teachers and parents alike.

Conclusion:

Reading material selected from the Internet in this way will, by definition, be of interest to the student as you have used the student's "interests" to select the material and it has been personalised in a manner that is easy to read and it is almost free!

Precaution:

Everyone is aware that there is unsuitable material on the Internet. However, there is also unsuitable material in books and magazines. Parents can use the same selection process with the computer as they would use with books. In addition, there is software available, which prohibits students mis-using the Internet, which can be purchased at suitable computer software suppliers.

Some students want to read relevant sections in the newspaper but the newspaper print seems too small for them to be able to read. Is there anything I can do about this?

If you have a scanner connected to your computer simply scan the text into the word processor programme. Increase the font size of the letters and increase the line spacing to double line spacing, as outlined above. When you print out the document it will be in a much easier format for the student to read. Imagine a student with dyslexia being able to read all about his favourite football team. I have found scanning in football stories from the popular type newspapers most beneficial. The English used in such newspapers is easy to read and the student wants to read it.

Scrap album

This was an idea that was fashionable when I was young and I have used it to interest students in reading. Some students have compiled scrap albums of their favourite football team or football heroes. In this way they are able to read and re-read the same material time and time again and yet they seem to do so without any loss of novelty. Other students have compiled scrap albums from magazines covering such interests as fashion, motorcars, pop music, sports etc.

Can you imagine asking a student with dyslexia to prepare thirty or forty pages about a certain topic? By using the scrap album idea, students not only are able to carry out this task but also do it with great interest. Very often you will also find them reading the information in each other's scrap albums.

Conclusion:

It is crucial to have reading material that a student wants to read. When you pick up a newspaper you only read the parts of a newspaper that interest you. For a student with dyslexia, the most important criteria for selecting reading material, is that the student is interested in the material that he/she is reading!

Chapter 15

Paired reading

What is the function of paired reading?

When a child learns any new skill it is usually with the help of a parent or somebody who is a master of that skill; for example, learning to ride a bicycle, learning to kick a football, learning how to skip or an adult learning to drive. In the same way, reading is a skill, which is best learned when working with someone who is a skilled reader. After all, for many jobs we often use the phrase that two heads are better than one. In Victorian days they used a monitor system in a classroom whereby one child was taught to read a passage, who then sat with his peers and taught the same passage to several of his peers so it is certainly not a new idea.

There seems to be two ways to teach; an exact way, when we teach step by step and a generalised way, when we teach all steps together. Imagine trying to teach a young child how to ride the bicycle in the following manner:

We would explain that the bicycle is an unstable object. If the bicycle starts to fall to the left we should lean to the right and vice versa. To turn the bicycle to the left, we should pull the left handlebar towards us and push the right handlebar away from us and vice versa to turn to the right. At the same time to make the bicycle go forward we should move our legs in a circular fashion pushing the pedals. When we want to stop the bicycle we should pull the brake levers towards us to activate the brake blocks. Of course this would be a ridiculous way to teach and would end up with a frustrated teacher and a frustrated child who would still be unable to ride the bicycle.

A more successful way to teach would be to hold onto the saddle and walk quickly beside the cyclist, as they learn to steer and pedal. We do not expect the cyclist to have balancing skills immediately. As we hold onto the bicycle for a period of time the cyclist becomes more and more confident so that they can retain their balance for longer and longer periods of time. We do not let go of the saddle until we are confident the cyclist will not fall off. Even then we let go of the saddle in such a way that the cyclist is not aware that we have in fact let go! It is only after a period of time when the cyclist has gained sufficient confidence that we let them know that we are letting go of the saddle! Hey presto – within a short period of time the cyclist has learned to ride a bicycle!

If we were to try to teach someone how to cycle by walking very, very slowly, one step slowly after another, it would be much more difficult for the cyclist to learn the skill of balance. In fact the faster the cyclist is allowed to cycle, the quicker and easier it is to learn to balance. Also, if we distract the cyclist by talking about things other than cycling, again the cyclist learns to balance even more quickly. It seems that, when the cyclist is conscious of all the things that he/she is doing wrong and concentrating on how difficult it is to balance, the slower the cyclist seems to learn! However, when we distract the cyclist from the difficulties of balance, steering properly with the handlebars and moving the feet around in a circular fashion, the cyclist learns all of these skills at an unconscious level, much more quickly.

Similar principles apply to teaching a child to read. If we read each individual word slowly and deliberately and spend a long time trying to get the student to sound out each individual sound in the word, it takes a long time for the student to learn to read! However, if we adopt an approach to paired reading which emphasises a reasonably quick rate of reading and we only correct those words which the student is either incapable of identifying or identifies incorrectly, the student can learn to read in a relatively quick time!

Please remember that when most people read a book they do not necessarily read every word correctly or pronounce every word perfectly. How many times have you read a book involving a foreign character or characters? If the characters were Polish, for example, would you go to a Polish dictionary and look up the correct word to find out how to pronounce it perfectly in Polish? Would you think it necessary to go to a Polish evening class to learn how to pronounce Polish perfectly before reading a book in English about Polish characters? Of course not! Nobody is perfect! If we read a novel, which describes a room in detail, and we do not recognise a certain item of furniture in the description, do we stop reading and reach for the dictionary or give up the book and say that is too difficult to read? No, we just skip over that bit and continue reading. Why oh why, do we expect perfection from students reading books when we ourselves are not "perfect readers"?

Conditions for successful paired reading

Select suitable reading material, *(see Chapter 14)*.

Find a quiet comfortable place that is free from distractions, such as television or brothers or sisters.

Establish a fixed time each day that suits both the reader and the student so that reading becomes a daily routine.

Ensure the level of lighting is correct. We are all aware of when it is too dark to read. However, the light can also be too bright *(see Chapter 12 Visual dyslexia)* and please remember that it is easier to read with a normal incandescent bulb than a fluorescent tube.

Make sure the seating is comfortable and that both the reader and the student can see the book and follow the text easily.

Have a light yellow coloured highlighter and, if you are right-handed, sit on the right-hand side of the student. When you reach across to highlight a word the student is able to see easily the word you are highlighting! Vice versa if you are a left-hand reader.

Please remember the idea behind paired reading is to enable the student to learn to read relatively quickly and, like learning to ride a bicycle, the student practises reading with your help until they are able to read independently. Do not expect perfection and do not hold the student up by demanding perfection!

Steps in implementing paired reading

1. Ask the student why he/she wants to read the book, magazine or comic. The student should be able to recognise most words in the material. If the student has difficulty in recognising more than one word in ten, the reading material is not suitable!

2. Decide on a length of time for reading which suits both the reader and the student.

3. Decide on the use of "signals". Perhaps a tap on the back of the reader's hand will signify that the student wants to read on their own. Perhaps the student touching the top right-hand corner of the book will signify that he/she wants the reader to read along with him/her.

4. Tell the student that you and he/she are going to read aloud together. When the student wants to read on his/her own just use the agreed signal and then the student can read on his or her own. Another method of achieving the same result is for the reader to progressively lower the tone of their voice so that the student becomes the dominant voice.

5. Start reading the passage and if the student mis-reads a word, just highlight the word and pronounce it. Next, have the student repeat the word and carry on together reading from that word. Wait for the student's signal and then the student will read on his/her own, or lower your voice progressively. (This is much the same method of teaching as when teaching to ride a bicycle. When the person who is learning to cycle starts to lose their balance we adjust the balance by holding the back of the saddle until they are confident and re-establish their own balance but we do not let go of the saddle immediately, we allow the cyclist to get their confidence back first.)

6. The important three P's:

Praise, Praise, Praise. There is no better method of encouragement or building self-esteem within the student than by using words of praise such as: "well done", "great", "that's even better", "I am delighted with your progress today" etc. and do not forget that the opposite is also true. The reader should never raise his/her voice, sigh in exasperation, or give any other negative signal.

7. When you have finished reading the passage, go back to the highlighted words and identify them again for the student. Ask the student to then identify the words as you point them out in random order. Do not expect 100% accuracy. In fact, remember that if the student recognises one third of the words then his/her ability to read words has increased!

8. When you have finished reading the passage, it is a good idea to ask the student to explain in his/her own words what the passage was about. After all this is what reading is all about: one person has an idea in their head, which may or not be a story, which they then write down. A second person reads the written words and forms a picture in their head of what they have read. So, the mechanics of reading and writing are that one person has an idea in their head and writes it down; the second person, after reading what the first person has written, then has the same idea in their head. The main thrust of reading and writing is the transfer of an idea from one person's head to another person's head without both people being present. *(See Chapter 6 on comprehension).* It is not necessary to have every word correctly written down or correctly read in order for this to happen. Encourage people to read, to achieve knowledge or simply for pure enjoyment .... Don't expect them to be word perfect!

9. Over a period of time at the end of the paired reading session you can ask the student to look back over previous sessions of reading. Ask the student to note how the number of highlighted words is diminishing over time. This indeed is a great "convincer" for the student that he/she is making progress. Point out also, that words that were highlighted in previous sessions can now be read. Not only does this give the student a sense of achievement but it also shows that the highlighting method has a function and that it works!

Please note: for students who have very poor reading skills, especially adults, the above method of paired reading can be modified:

Ask the student to look at the passage and to highlight in a light colour other than yellow, e.g. orange, all of the words that they recognise. Next ask the student to just read all of the orange highlighted words ignoring all words that are not highlighted. At each full stop ask the student whether he can make "sense" of what he is reading, and do not interrupt the student's explanation. Encourage the student to guess and praise his/her understanding of the passage. Students with very poor reading ability are often of the opinion that they have to read every word or else they cannot read at all. Getting over this barrier, using this method very quickly shifts the student from a "can't read" to a "might be able to read" frame of mind.

Demonstration:

Pick up a newspaper and highlight every second word from a section of the paper that you would normally read. Now just read the highlighted words and see whether you understand what you have read. You will be surprised at the results. You will not understand every last detail but you will get an overview of the story. Please remember reading and writing is the transfer of one person's idea to another person, not necessarily identifying every word correctly.

Most people have learned to ride a bicycle. Imagine if the person who taught you to ride a bicycle had used the following method. How would you have felt.

A bicycle is very unsteady and you will probably fall off. When you fall on the ground it will be very, very hard and you will probably hit your head and get a large cut and lots of blood will flow. There may be so much blood that we will have to call an ambulance to take you to hospital. In the hospital you might have to have lots and lots of stitches, which will be very sore. Now get up on the bicycle and learn to ride it!

This of course seems preposterous, but how many parents have tried to encourage their children to read by pointing out all the negative things that will happen in their life if they do not learn to read. Furthermore, it is not enough to try to motivate a child to learn to read by saying that they will enjoy school so much more. The adult may well understand this but the child who is having difficulty reading in school may not be open to this suggestion. It is so much better to point out all the good things which reading opens up. Reading a book can be a wonderful experience, reading comics is really great, reading magazines about your favourite sport or interest, sending text messages is more than fun, writing e-mails to your friends is really amusing and of course surfing on the web allows you to read any thing that interests you!

ALWAYS FINISH A READING SESSION ON A POSITIVE NOTE!!!!!

Paired reading .... two heads are better than one as long as they are smiling!

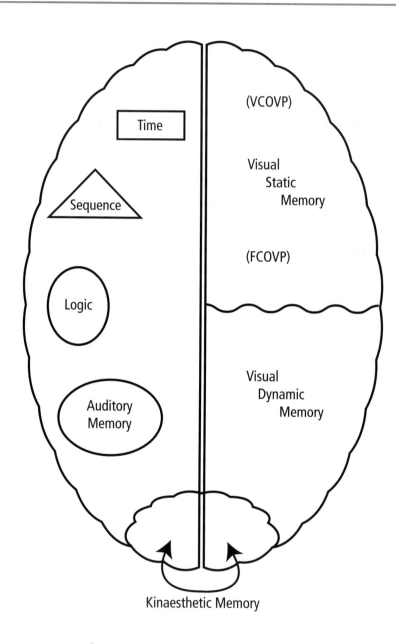

Diagram 16.1   Dyslexia@bay™ Model of the brain

Chapter 16

The dyslexia@bay™ model of the brain

How does our brain work and what is different about how the brain of a person with dyslexia works?

The importance of the dyslexia@bay ™ model of the brain is that it can be used to explain the difficulties and behaviour of individuals with dyslexia and can also be used to predict their thought processes and hence their behaviour. Most importantly the model can be used to identify interventions, which can minimise the symptoms exhibited by each individual with dyslexia.

What do we mean by the word 'model'?

In today's modern technological world we use cars, telephones, video recorders, computers etc. all sophisticated technical devices, many of which were unheard of even 100 years ago. We can use these machines easily and effortlessly because we have a model in our head of how they work.

Most people jump into a car several times each day and drive to work, the supermarket, school etc., without knowing exactly how a car works. We know that when we turn the steering wheel, the front wheels change direction. We know that when we press the accelerator, the car will go faster because more petrol goes into the engine. We know that when we press the brake pedal, the car slows down. We have a model in our brain of how the car works. It is not important that we understand every last detail of how a car engine works. It does not make a difference that we do not understand how friction works in the brakes. It does not matter that we fully understand what happens to the petrol in the engine. What is important is that we have a model in our brain of how the car works, which enables us to drive the car. It does not matter whether this model is absolutely true or not. The important thing is that the model is simple enough for us to understand and use, so that we can drive the car easily.

It is of great value to have a model of how the brain works to enable us to understand what is different about how the brain of a person with dyslexia works. The dyslexia@bay ™ model of the brain described in this chapter is simple, easy to understand and easy to use by students, parents and teachers. By using this model we can understand how people think differently and, in particular, how people with dyslexia think. Furthermore, it should also enable us to predict the future thinking strategies of a person who has dyslexia.

The model that follows does not use the technical names of the parts or locations of the brain as this could cause more confusion than understanding. Furthermore, the model does not claim to be "the truth". However, by understanding the model, you will have a better understanding of the thinking strategies of people who have dyslexia.

Models, which have subsequently proved to be "wrong", can still be useful and used successfully. At one time the world was considered to be flat but man discovered how to navigate round this world. This was before Columbus discovered that the world was in fact round and that the 'flat' model was 'wrong'. However, we still use flat maps to navigate when driving a car in unfamiliar territory. Ships still use flat charts to navigate all around the world. A model does not have to be true to be useful!

When electricity was first discovered it was decided that the direction of the current would be from positive to negative. However, this was later found to be the opposite of the "truth". Even to this day, the direction of electric current shown in all diagrams in schools, colleges and places of research and development, is based on the model of the current flowing in the wrong direction. This model is still used because it is useful.

The hexagon with a circle in the middle of it does not fully describe the benzene ring but it is still the model used for formulating all our pharmaceutical drugs and oil products. The model is not "true" but it is useful.

The diagram shown at the beginning of this chapter is a simple visual representation of what follows. It should be emphasised that the diagram is just a representation of the model and is not intended to imply that there are actual physical locations responsible for each individual thought process. It is the interlinking of various aspects of the brain, which produces the different thought processes.

How does memory work?

The brain is essentially a device, which takes in information through our eyes, ears, nose, skin and tongue, which make up our five senses. This information is then stored in our memory in various locations. Once this information is stored in our various memory locations it affects our behaviour and also how we store information in the future.

Think of a young child walking along on a lovely summer's day, with blue skies and sunshine, and her parents take her to an ice-cream shop for the very first time. The child's eyes are excited by all the colours of the different flavours of ice cream: the bright pink of the strawberry, the cream colour of the vanilla, the dark brown colour of chocolate, the bright green of the lime etc. The assistant then places two or three scoops into the biscuit cone and sprinkles some chocolate flakes on top. The parent hands the ice cream to the child. First of all there is a look of surprise and delight on the child's face and then a look of shock when her lips touch the cold ice cream. After being encouraged by her parents to continue eating the ice cream and listening to her parents using words like "yummy" and "mmmmmm", the child learns to appreciate the taste of ice cream.

What has happened in the child's brain?

Firstly, information was taken in through the eyes, the different colours of the ice cream. These colours were remembered in the part of the brain called the visual memory. Next the child tasted the ice cream and that taste was recorded in the part of the brain called the taste memory. Both the texture and the coldness of the ice cream were stored in different areas of the part of the brain, the touch memory and the temperature memory.

When the parents mentioned the words "yummy" and "mmmmmm" they were stored in the auditory memory (where we remember sounds and words). This latter part of the memory is quite interesting. Children normally do not enjoy the initial taste of ice cream, as it is often too cold for them. This is much the same as adults who taste alcohol for the first time; they rarely enjoy the taste initially. However, the parents have probably use the words "yummy" and "mmmmmm" on previous occasions when the child was enjoying herself enormously. From those earlier experiences the child has learned to associate enjoyable events with those words. Hence the child learned to enjoy ice cream by using the words "yummy" and "mmmmmm" which had been associated with pleasurable events in the past. How many adults can truly claim to have enjoyed alcohol on first tasting? However, by being in the company of others who enjoyed drinking alcohol, we learned to "appreciate" the "taste" of alcohol. The memory may be stored in the brain but the opinion of the memory varies.

Demonstration:

Remember a very special meal that you really enjoyed, perhaps a special Christmas dinner. Close your eyes and make a vivid picture in your mind of that meal. Think of how the meat looked and tasted and the texture of it on your tongue. Think of the colour of the vegetables, the taste and the texture. Remember the look and taste of each course of the meal. Remember also the happy and excited voices of others who were at the meal. Recall your feelings - happiness, contentment, excitement etc. Go through each of your senses with that memory: what you saw, what you heard, what you smelled, what you tasted and how you felt.

If your memories have been really vivid you will indeed sense the pleasure of the Christmas dinner yet again!

How does memory affect behaviour?

Returning to our story of the child and the ice cream, the next time the child passes the same shop she will of course remember the previous experience and, if she has another ice cream, it will reinforce the memory of the first visit. After visiting the ice cream shop several times the child then learns to "encourage" the parents to visit the ice cream shop by changing her behaviour. The child may become well behaved, smiling, pleading and even devious so that she can get to visit the ice cream shop again!

What has happened in the child's brain to explain this change in behaviour?

When the child passes the ice cream shop she recalls seeing it before in her visual memory. This triggers her visual memory of the colours of the ice cream and the picture of the ice cream in the biscuit cone with the chocolate flakes sprinkled on top. This in turn, triggers the memory of the taste of the ice cream as well as the coldness and the texture of the ice cream. Of course the words "yummy" and "mmmmmm" are also triggered in her auditory memory. It is truly amazing that all of these different memories, stored in different locations in the brain, come together to form one large intricate memory.

After several visits to the ice cream shop the child does not even have to pass the shop to trigger the memories. Blue skies and a warm sunny day may trigger the memory of the coolness of the ice cream. The child's parent may have used the word "yummy" in an unrelated context and that one memory may be sufficient to trigger all the other memories associated with ice cream. Perhaps the child has touched cold metal railings and associates the memory of coldness with the memory of cold ice cream. Perhaps the child sees an advertisement for ice cream and that sets off the chain of memories associated with ice cream.

The human brain has the capacity to recall one memory and, at the same time, all the other memories associated with that memory. Obviously when the child recalls one memory of ice cream, it triggers all the other memories associated with ice cream. Once these memories come together, the child has the "idea of ice cream" in her head. Once this idea of ice cream is in her head it drives her behaviour and she will "encourage" her parents to buy her an ice cream. She will use previous memories of when she was well behaved, smiling, pleading and even devious in order that she may visit the ice cream shop!

Demonstration:

The advertising industry really understands interlinked and associated memories. Remember an advert for a particular food you enjoy and consider how each of the five senses is being triggered!

We have five basic types of memory:

Visual memory (what we see)

Auditory memory (what we hear)

Olfactory memory (what we smell)

Taste memory (what we taste)

Kinaesthetic memory (what we touch or feel)

The dyslexia@bay ™ model of the brain is primarily concerned with visual memory and auditory memory.

Do we have different types of visual memory?

The dyslexia@bay™ model of the brain identifies 114 types of visual memory, which fall into two basic categories of visual memory – **Visual Static Memory** and **Visual Dynamic Memory** - and as you will see below there are many different types within each category.

Visual Static Memory

Demonstration:

If we remember standing outside the house we grew up in, we can recall how many windows were in front of the house, what colour the front door was, how many steps were outside the front door, if any, what colour the walls were, what colour the roof was etc. We can remember this picture or image in our head in many different ways:

Two-dimensional picture

Three-dimensional picture

Colour picture

Black-and-white picture

Cartoon picture

The human brain is amazing in the sense that we can take a visual memory and manipulate it. We often refer to people having a great "imagination"; hence, it is not really surprising that the word imagination is derived from the word "image". There are many, many more ways in which the human brain can take an image and either re-form it or manipulate it. If we consider all of these pictures to be a type of photograph or still image, we can refer to this form of memory as Visual Static Memory. That is to say that it is visually based and also that the images are stationary as in a photograph.

Demonstration:

Imagine standing and looking at your car, which is parked outside your home. You can view the car either from the side, the front or the rear. You will have an image in your mind, which may or may not be two-dimensional, and you will be viewing that image from a fixed stationary position in your mind, which we refer to as your **Fixed Centre Of Visual Perception (FCOVP).**

Most people view typed or written letters, written on the page as two-dimensional images on a flat screen or page. Because these two dimensional letters are viewed from one fixed position, these letters appear to be the same each time they are viewed or read. When viewing letters as two-dimensional images from a Fixed Centre Of Visual Perception, then the letters appear to be the same from minute to minute, hour to hour, and day to day. There is only one memory of each letter and word for the brain to remember and recognise.

This type of image remembered in the brain is a static image viewed from a fixed position.

Demonstration:

Imagine looking at your car again but this time notice what colour the car is, look inside and note the colour of the upholstery, note the colour of the dashboard and the steering wheel. Imagine the boot or trunk is open and look inside to see the colour of the floor covering. Next imagine walking round to the front of the car and examine what colour the front bumper or fender is.

You will have different images of the car in your mind, which you will be viewing from different perceptual (or body) positions. You will have moved your Centre of Visual Perception by imagining yourself moving around the car and examining it from inside, the rear and the front. However, your Centre of Visual Perception will still be in a fixed position relative to your body.

By imagining the car from various perceptual positions in this way, we tend to perceive a three-dimensional image in our mind. When we refer back to the memory of the car in this way we have a variety of inter-linking memories of the car, which tend to make the total memory three-dimensional. Would it be easier for you to recognise your own car from the side, the front, the rear, the top or the bottom? One thing that would be certain is that we would not all agree!

Diagram 16.2

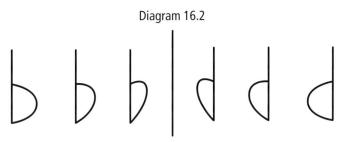

Varying angles of visual perception

However, imagine a student viewing the letter "b" as a three-dimensional image, from the front, the side, the back, the top and the bottom. The following are the images he would perceive:

It easy to understand how confusion arises for such a student when trying to recognise the letter 'b' because he will have different memories of various different images of the letter 'b' stored in different locations in his brain. He may well recognise the letter "b" one day but perhaps not the next day or one hour but not the next hour. How difficult is it for a child to learn his/her letters if the letters are viewed three-dimensionally from different perceptual positions at different times?

There are a few students who have the ability to perceive three-dimensional objects quite differently in that their Centre of Visual Perception is not fixed but can move relative to their body – they have a **Variable Centre of Visual Perception (VCOVP).** Such students can view the letter "b" from in front of the page as the vast majority of people do but they can also view the letter from "behind" the page with the result that the letter "b" looks as if it is the letter "d"! We have found that there are many reasons why children mix up the letters "b" and "d". This is only one of them and we shall discover others elsewhere in the book e.g. clockwise and anti-clockwise dominance.

Visual Dynamic Memory

There is another family of visual images, which the dyslexia@bay ™ model of the brain refers to as Visual Dynamic Memory. These images are moving images like those we see at the movies or on television. The interesting thing about these images is that not only are they moving, but they also have associated sounds.

Demonstration:

Imagine getting behind the wheel of the car and driving to the local supermarket or place of work. You may envisage driving from your home and turning either left or right, maybe stopping at some traffic lights, perhaps joining a major road junction, or driving underneath a bridge etc. When you imagine this journey you create a film or movie in your mind.

This type of visual memory is different from Visual Static Memory because the images are moving and there may be sounds associated with the movie. We refer to this type of visual memory as Visual Dynamic Memory.

Demonstration:

Imagine approaching traffic lights and seeing someone approaching from the side and not waiting for the red light. There may be the sound of a horn or perhaps the sound of skidding tyres on the ground.

Such sounds are not associated with Visual Static Memory, which only sees photographs or still pictures.

Summary of Visual Memory

(a) Visual Static Memory

Memory of images that are stationary as in a photograph.

Such images can be viewed from one location i.e. from a Fixed Centre Of Visual Perception.

Example: Imagine standing outside your house and looking at the front from one spot.

Such images can also be viewed from various locations i.e. from a number of Fixed Centres Of Visual Perception.

Example: Imagine walking around your house and viewing your house from many angles so that you examine the front, the sides and the rear and even the top of the house.

(b) Visual Dynamic Memory:

Memory of images that are viewed as a moving picture as in a movie/video.

Some of these moving images we see in our mind do not have any sounds associated with the image.

Some of these moving images we see our mind do have associated sounds such as voices or background noise.

How do Visual Static and Visual Dynamic Memory interact?

If we imagine a journey to or from work in the car using our Visual Dynamic Memory we can of course stop the movie at any point. We can freeze frame the image and hence think of that part of the journey as a photograph or still image using our Visual Static Memory.

Demonstration:

Think of your journey going to or from work and think of one particular landmark that you pass. The landmark could be a particular road junction, a set of traffic lights, a particular house, or particular shop. Stop the movie at that point and freeze-frame the landmark. You can look at the particular landmark and continue viewing the landmark from inside the car. You have now switched from a Visual Dynamic Memory to a Visual Static Memory and are viewing your landmark from a Fixed Centre of Visual Perception. Now imagine that you have parked the car at the landmark and get out of the car and walk around it. View the landmark from all sides. Now you have taken the memory and viewed the memory from different perceptual positions.

We are able to take the memory of driving the car to work from a Visual Dynamic Memory location and transfer it to a Visual Static Memory location viewed from a single perceptual position and further to transfer it to a Visual Static Memory location viewed from different perceptual positions.

In summary, when we perceive an image with our eyes, we use our visual memory to remember that image and we store the visual memory in one or more different locations within our memory. Subsequently, we can use our visual memory to recreate the image and view it from different perspectives, simply by recalling memories of the image stored in the various locations within visual memory.

Logic and time

How do we think logically?

As you will see below, Visual Dynamic Memory plays a key role in enabling us to think logically and sequentially according to the dyslexia@bay™ model of the brain.

Demonstration:

Imagine you live in a home with a small garden outside the front door. Imagine standing at the front door. You can see a lawn about four metres long, which needs to be mowed. At the end of the lawn is a flowerbed, one metre wide, with flowers and weeds growing in it. At the back of the flowerbed grows a hedge, about one metre high that needs to be trimmed.

Ask yourself what would be the logical order in which to mow the grass, weed the flowerbed and trim the hedge?

If you trim the hedge first, all the trimmings will fall on the flowerbed and you will be unable to weed the flowerbed without removing the trimmings first. So the logical thing to do is to weed the flowerbed first and then trim the hedge and allow the trimmings to fall upon the flowerbed. You could then use a rake to remove both the trimmings from the hedge and the weeds and put them into a bag. Inevitably some of the trimmings from the hedge and weeds from the flowerbed will find their way onto the lawn. This does not matter, as we will use the lawn mower not only to cut the grass, but also to mow up the hedge trimmings and weeds that have fallen onto the lawn.

You have used your Visual Dynamic Memory to work out, in a logical fashion, the order in which you should carry out the above tasks. You were able to do this because you could use your Visual Dynamic Memory and freeze-frame each section of the video/movie in your imagination, thus tackling the task in a logical sequence.

In fact we use our Visual Dynamic Memory on an everyday basis to enable us to carry out tasks in a logical order.

Demonstration:

Examine the following list of tasks and put them in a logical order so that they will require the least amount of time and effort:

Drive home from work

Collect the clothes from the dry cleaners

Buy a newspaper and magazine at the newsagent

Purchase some groceries at the supermarket

Fill the car with petrol

When you have completed this exercise take a pencil and write the numbers 1 to 5 beside each task. The numbers will obviously vary from reader to reader depending upon the geography and layout of where they live.

What mental processes did you use? Did you use a movie/video in your head? Did you imagine some still pictures? Were you able to rearrange the order of the still pictures and form a continuous movie/video in your head? Did you work out a logical sequence such that you would not backtrack over the same route and thus save time and effort.

We use our visual memory, both Visual Dynamic Memory (movie/video) and Visual Static Memory (photograph) to carry out our everyday tasks in a logical fashion in order to save ourselves time and effort.

How many times have we arrived home and forgotten one task on the way and had to retrace our journey. Very often we say to ourselves "If only I had taken the time to think it through, I would have saved myself so much time!" Let us consider next what "time" is and how it is related to logic within the dyslexia@bay ™ model of our brain?

How exactly does our brain store time?

Time in our brain has two attributes, firstly how much time has passed and secondly the order of events, which comes first and which comes last.

In considering the passage of time, how do we know how much time has passed, whether it is five minutes, thirty five minutes or an hour and five minutes? We all seem to sense when a task is easier than we thought, in that we completed it in less time than we anticipated. We also sense when a task has taken too much time and the sense of frustration that goes with this. So how does our brain sense fast and slow.

Let us return to the previous exercise involving the tasks carried out in the garden. We used our Visual Dynamic Memory to organise trimming the hedge, weeding the flowerbed and mowing the lawn. We simply made a movie/video in our imagination. If we were to actually carry out those tasks then we could either do the task physically more quickly than the movie/video in our imagination and hence a task would be easier than we "thought". However, if the task was carried out more slowly than the movie/video in our imagination then we would sense that the tasks were much more difficult than we had anticipated and a sense of frustration would ensue. The last possibility is that we would carry out the tasks at the same speed as the movie/video in our imagination in which case, when asked, we would indicate that the task took the same amount of time as we had expected.

In the world of sport, athletes and sportsmen/women are often coached to visualise the event before they actually carry it out. People who play golf are encouraged to visualise the shape and range of the shot before they play it. Athletes at a high jump see themselves successfully making the jump in their mind's eye before actually jumping. Sprinters are trained to see and feel the 100 m in their mind before they actually get into a starting position.

Case study:

Graham competes in canoe slalom, an event in which visualisation is crucial to success. No two courses are the same and white water, by its very nature, is continuously changing. Actual practices on the water are not allowed so that the only way to prepare for an event is to visualise you performing the run from start to finish and negotiating all the gates in between.

The aim of visualisation is not only to make a video or movie in your head using Visual Dynamic Memory but also to do so in the exact time you expect it will take to complete the run.

In a particular event Graham recalls needing to trim five seconds off his first run time in his second run. In between runs he 'practised' by making a movie of himself performing the second run five seconds quicker and when he came to do his second run for real he achieved his goal of reducing his time by five seconds. Moreover, when re-running the movie of that second run at home that evening he did so in exactly the time it had taken earlier in the day.

This is a good example of the link between our sense of time passing and the use of our Visual Dynamic Memory.

What do we mean by sequencing and what exactly do the words "before" and "after" mean with respect to time?

The words "before" and "after" refer to the order or sequence of events with respect to time.

Demonstration:

Recall the everyday shopping exercise that you carried out earlier. Did you fill the car with petrol before you purchased the groceries or afterwards? Did you buy the newspaper before you collected the clothes from the dry cleaners or afterwards?

We can answer these questions quite easily by running a video/movie in our Visual Dynamic Memory, stopping it at the relevant points and using our Visual Static Memory to examine the individual events as photographs. This is the process by which we learn to "sequence", the implications of which are described in the Chapter 8 on sequencing.

We can now appreciate how our brain senses how much time has passed and also how our brain interprets "before" and "after". However, if for some reason we do not fully access our Visual Dynamic Memory or all aspects of our Visual Static Memory then we do not interpret time in the same way as others who have full access.

Imagine not being able to access your Visual Dynamic Memory and having no appreciation of the passing of time. Suppose that you work in a job where there is no definite finishing time. After arriving at nine o'clock in the morning you start work, lunchtime passes, as does five o'clock in the evening. Seven o'clock comes and goes, nine o'clock comes and goes and you still have no idea how much time has passed and when you will be finishing. How frustrated would you feel working day in and day out with such a regime?

For some people with dyslexia, this is their world. Imagine sitting down at your desk to do homework each evening and having no idea how long it is likely to take, whether you are doing it quickly or slowly or whether you have just started or have nearly finished!

Auditory memory

We use auditory memory on a regular basis. Every time we talk to ourselves and give ourselves "messages" to remember we are in fact using our auditory memory. For example, I must remember to have the car serviced,

I must remember to fill the car up with petrol, I must remember to purchase those groceries on the way home, I must remember to buy this month's golf magazine etc. It is not important that we remember these items for the rest of our life so there is no point in putting them in our long-term memory. Hence we just remember these everyday activities in our short-term memory.

If we wish to transfer something from our auditory short-term memory to our visual long-term memory we talk to ourselves and the same time we make a picture in our head to describe our "self talk".

How many times has someone asked us the name of somebody and we reply "I know that name; it is on the tip of my tongue. I can see her face; the name will come to me in a minute!" This is a typical example of being able to recall a picture of a face from our visual memory and unable to recall the name from our short-term auditory memory.

The brain essentially works by various aspects of our memory working together! When one or two aspects of that memory are not working to their full potential then that thinking process will be inefficient. Whether it is remembering letters or words either while writing or reading, the thinking process will not be complete.

Kinaesthetic memory

This is the memory of touch, feel and movement. Once we learn to swim then it is almost impossible to forget. We may not have been swimming for many years but as soon as we hit the water our body starts to swim without thinking. We may not have ridden a bicycle for many years but, after a minute or two, once we are astride a bicycle off we go! In the same way we can learn the spelling of a word by saying the letters to ourselves a number of times, making a picture of the spelling in our visual memory and writing it out several times to get the "feeling" of the spelling.

Demonstration:

Take a blank sheet of paper and write three sentences describing the front of the house that you were born in.

What mental processes are involved in this exercise?

We first make a picture in our imagination that is drawn from our visual memory and then we use our auditory memory to describe the picture in our head. We then write down the words by using a synthesis of the visual recollection of what the word looks like from our visual memory and what the word feels like from our kinaesthetic memory. We are indeed very complex creatures!

If all aspects of our memory - auditory, visual and kinaesthetic - are not working or not working together, the simple process of writing down the sentence becomes highly laborious. The resulting sentences will be accompanied by incorrect spellings, devoid of colourful adjectives and certainly without punctuation. *(See Chapter 7 on writing difficulties).*

This is not to say that the mind trying to collect these memories from the various aspects of the brain is in any way limited. What is limited is the access to these memories. Once the student is taught how to access the memories then indeed the mind can produce in written form the results of the great ideas of the mind! Please read Chapter 19 "Famous people who have/had dyslexia" which documents those famous people who have/had dyslexia and who are known/remembered for their deeds, talents and great minds!

Summary: The dyslexia@bay™ model of the brain.

A model of the brain does not necessarily have to be "true" to be useful in explaining the behaviour of a person with dyslexia.

A thought process involves the interlinking of various "aspects" of the brain rather than occurring in an individual part of the brain.

The various aspects of the dyslexia@bay™ model of brain are as follows:

Visual Memory

Visual Static Memory

Memory of images that are stationary as in a photograph.

Some of these images will be viewed from one location and we say that these images are viewed from a Fixed Centre Of Visual Perception. The image may be two or three-dimensional.

Example: Standing outside your house and looking at the front from one spot.

Some of these images will be viewed from various locations and will tend to be three-dimensional.

Example: Walking around your house and viewing your house from many angles so that you examine the front, the sides and the rear and even the top of the house.

Visual Dynamic Memory

Memory of images that are viewed as a moving picture as in a movie/video

These moving images we see in our mind may or may not have associated sounds such as voices or background noise.

Auditory memory

Kinaesthetic memory

Logic

Sequence

Time

The significance of the dyslexia@bay™ model is that it can be used to explain the mental strategies and resulting behaviour and difficulties of individuals with dyslexia. Most importantly the model can be used to identify interventions, which can minimise the symptoms of dyslexia.

Please note that difficulties associated with the eye movements of those who have dyslexia are dealt with in Chapter 5. It is hoped that the reader, having read the entire book, will integrate these difficulties within the model. After all, those images in the visual memory and sounds in the auditory memory can only arrive there in the first place having been seen by the eyes or heard by the ears and whatever distortion is caused by the eyes or ears or the pathways connecting them to the brain.

Chapter 17

Educational Psychologist's report

In the normal course of events, a student's "learning difference" is noticed either by the teacher or by the parent at home. The teacher will become aware that the child is performing well orally in the classroom but seems to be under-performing in written tasks or reading. Frequently, a parent who is working with the student at home notices that the student has difficulty when tackling homework. The parent may become aware that, at an early age, the child appears to be "reading" but, in actual fact, has learned to read the page off by heart. When the parent points to individual words the child has difficulty recognising those words. There are a lot of other symptoms of dyslexia mentioned in Chapter 3 "What are the signs and symptoms of dyslexia" that can be readily identified by both parents and teachers

There are many reasons why a student may not be learning at the rate expected by the teacher or parent and some of these are listed below. It is very important for the parent to inform the teacher of any aspect of the student's home life, which may affect the student's learning ability at school. The following aspects should be discussed with the teacher *before* the student is screened for a specific learning difficulty.

Intellectual and behavioural factors

The student may have a below average IQ and therefore may not be able to learn as quickly as his/her classmates.

Quite often a student who is spoken to, as an adult will pick up an adult vocabulary and phraseology and may seem to perform orally at a high level.

The student may have a normal IQ but have specific learning difficulties.

The student may have a poor attention span.

Physical factors

The student may not be getting enough sleep.

This may be due to environmental factors such as noise, the bedroom too warm etc.

The student may be worried about school, friends, classmates or something at home. There are lots of things that children "worry about", real or imagined.

The student may not be going to bed early enough. Different adults require different amounts of sleep and so do different children. Sometimes within a family one particular child may require more sleep than the others. Parents are only too aware that some children require less sleep than others in the family!

Health factors

The family doctor will have the medical history of the student and there may be implications within this for a child's learning ability. The doctor should be consulted at this stage informing him/her that an Educational Psychologist may assess the student.

The student may have missed school due to a serious illness or an ongoing illness. However, it often amazing how quickly children who have missed long periods of school can seem to "catch up" relatively easily within a short period of time.

Visual problems such as short sightedness can often go undetected. In many instances a teacher may request the student has an eyesight test because the student is having difficulty copying from the board in school. This is not to be confused with aspects of visual dyslexia or eye-tracking problems as previously referred to in Chapters 12 and 5.

The student may have hearing problems such as those associated with "glue ear" caused by infections in or malfunctioning of the Eustachian tubes.

These are tubes connecting the inner ear to the throat. (When flying we can cause our ears to "pop" by pinching the nose and blowing out, with lips closed, thus opening the Eustachian tubes.) This can lead to problems with sounding out words especially in the early years of school; high-pitched frequencies are affected most e.g. those associated with the slender vowels e and i.

Speech problems such as those associated with delayed development of language also cause problems in the classroom environment while attempting to learn letters or words by using a "sound" methodology.

A child may not be getting adequate nutrition. Because of the ready availability of food nowadays some children seem to snack regularly on unhealthy foods and eat relatively little at meal times. Because of the effects of advertising on the television etc. children will not normally select wholesome food of their own accord. There have been many cases when a child's performance has been greatly increased by use of a balanced nutritional diet. There is some evidence to indicate that some children's performance may be affected by taking Omega 3 Oils.

Emotional difficulties

Children sometimes have emotional difficulties associated with school, such as being bullied. Obviously this can greatly affect the learning ability of a student in the classroom. Perhaps there are other emotional difficulties in the home that are adding to these learning difficulties in the classroom? Parents should inform the teacher if there are any situations in the home environment, which could affect the child emotionally, either in the short-term, or the long-term in school.

Once all of the above factors have been ruled out, the parent and the teacher should proceed further. On agreement between the parent and the teacher, the student may be offered a Dyslexia Screening Test. This test can be offered to a child from the age of four and a half years upwards and may be performed by a teacher trained to use a specific Dyslexia Screening Test. It is not a full psychological assessment and only indicates whether a student may or may not have dyslexia. It is not a definitive test. However, if the Dyslexia Screening Test indicates that the student may have dyslexia then s/he should be recommended for a full psycho-educational assessment to be carried out by a qualified Educational Psychologist. It is important that the Educational Psychologist is recognised by the Department of Education, to ensure that s/he can benefit from recommended educational resources and provisions documented in the report. A list of Educational Psychologists should be obtained from the Department of Education before proceeding with an assessment.

How should I prepare my child for an Educational Psychologist's assessment?

Tell your child a few days before the appointment that it is going to take place so that they can get used to the idea.

Tell your child why you made the appointment and get agreement from the child that the appointment will be useful.

Perhaps offer the child a "treat" after the appointment has taken place.

Arrive at the Educational Psychologist's office thirty minutes before the appointment and take a short walk to allow the child to settle and get some fresh air. Arriving late for an appointment, getting caught in traffic or public transport being slow can cause the child to become stressed and this may affect his/her performance in the test.

Bring something the child likes to eat and drink before the appointment and perhaps after the appointment.

Explain to the child that you will be there to meet the Educational Psychologist but that you will not be present during the assessment. You will be waiting outside and will be there to greet the child after the appointment.

The Educational Psychologist's report

Each Educational Psychologist's report will be different. Each student being assessed will have different abilities and we would expect the reports to be different for each student. However, in addition, each country has different educational policies and the Educational Psychologist's report will also reflect these policies. Some Educational Psychologists are wary of labelling the student as either being dyslexic or having dyslexia as their opinion is that labelling a student may then induce the student to change his/her behaviour "to fit the label". Some Educational Psychologists may use phrases such as "tendencies of/towards dyslexia" or being "on the borderline of dyslexia".

The following are some of the more common aspects of a report but a report not containing all of these aspects will not necessarily be an incomplete report. Furthermore, there may well be additional aspects that an Educational Psychologist deems suitable to include for a particular student.

Relevant history:

This section will detail the student's siblings and his/her position in the family. The student's developmental history will be documented, indicating whether student crawled, walked and talked at expected milestones of development. It will contain the educational history of the student, listing chronologically which schools were attended. Parents' opinion of the progress within the school will be noted at this point, as will the teacher's remarks.

The purpose of the relevant history is to allow the reader to form an opinion as to why the student was referred for assessment. A student being assessed for dyslexia will perhaps be assessed every year or two and hence this section will also note any improvement or otherwise over a period of time.

Assessment:

How the student presented himself/herself at the assessment is noted. If the student has been cooperative, confident and of a content disposition during the test the results are more likely to be accurate. However, if the student has presented as being disinterested, uncooperative or restless the results of the test will be less accurate. It is important for the reader of the report to know whether the results are likely to reflect the true ability of the student.

Test results:

IQ results are expressed either as a percentage or as a percentile rank.

What does "percentile" mean?

Percentile rank figures provide a means of making a direct comparison with others in a similar category e.g. other 10 year olds. A score of 87th percentile means you are in the top 13 per cent of the people in that group for that particular test. In other words, in a group of 100 people in the same category, there are 87 people who are not as capable as you are.

An Educational Psychologist's report will include the student's intelligence quotient (IQ). This is necessary to determine whether the student is performing below his/her capability. It would be unfair to expect a student with a low IQ to perform beyond their capabilities.

An Educational Psychologist also assesses a student in order to identify the areas of strengths and weaknesses in their learning ability. Their report will detail the areas in which the student will need most help. The teacher, the school and the parent may use the report to design a suitable learning strategy for the student.

Whether you, or your child, have had an assessment, or you are contemplating having one, you will probably be aware of the difficulty in deciphering the written report given by an Educational Psychologist. This following Chapter attempts to explain a psychologist's report in layperson's terms. It is by no means a psychological debate on what defines intelligence or the use of psychometrics.

What is IQ?

IQ is an acronym for Intelligence Quotient. What constitutes intelligence has been a much-deliberated issue throughout the history of psychology.

Some of the earliest work in this field can be attributed to Alfred Binet at the beginning of the twentieth century. Binet, at the request of the French Government, devised a test to identify children who were too slow intellectually to benefit from a mainstream school curriculum. In 1905, Binet published a test consisting of a series of questions of increasing difficulty such that a bright child would answer questions in a category above his/her age group and a child who had lower intelligence than average would perform as a child of younger age. If a child answered all the questions for the seven-year-old category but not the eight-year-old category s/he was assigned a **mental age (MA) of** seven. This assigned mental age was compared to the actual or **chronological age (CA) of** the child to determine whether s/he was of low, average or high intelligence.

William Stern, a German psychologist, later devised the **intelligence quotient (IQ)** by expressing intelligence as a ratio of **mental age (MA) to chronological age (CA).**

$$\text{Intelligence Quotient IQ} = \frac{\text{Mental Age (MA)} \times 100}{\text{Chronological Age (CA)}}$$

This type of formula always results in an average IQ of 100 for any age group. An IQ greater than 100 indicates a higher than average intelligence and similarly an IQ of less than 100 indicates a lower than average intelligence. Subsequent IQ tests have maintained this notion.

Current IQ tests are designed to yield a normal distribution, or a bell-shaped curve, similar to differences in height by age or weight.

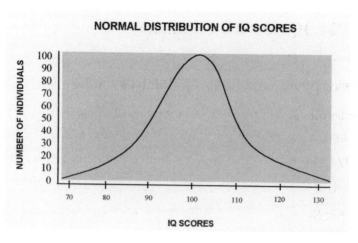

NORMAL DISTRIBUTION OF IQ SCORES

As you can see from this chart, 50% of the population have an IQ between 90 and 110 and this is considered to be 'average' (or normal). An IQ between 110 and 119 is considered to be above average, between 120 and 129 to be superior and above 130 gifted. If an IQ falls between 80 and 89, this is just below average, between 70 and 79 is borderline and below 69 indicates a learning disability.

Note:

It is important to remember that having a higher or lower IQ certainly does not make one a better or worse member of society, or a more valuable or less valuable person. IQ reflects only one aspect of a person. A moderately high IQ may be necessary for success in some fields. However, successful people often have a capacity for original thought that IQ tests do not assess.

Howard Gardner and others have developed theories and practice regarding various types of intelligence or multiple intelligences e.g. linguistic intelligence, musical intelligence, logical-mathematical intelligence, spatial intelligence, bodily-kinaesthetic intelligence and personal intelligences. These types of intelligences are not necessarily measured in a standard IQ test.

Intelligence tests are continually being revised, improved and updated. Psychologists do not claim that intelligence tests are an accurate science but they do refer to confidence limits of around 90%.

What is the IQ test most commonly used and how do I understand it and make use of it?

The Wechsler Intelligence Scale for Children (WISC-III)

This is the test most commonly used by psychologists worldwide to test a child's IQ and to examine the strengths and weaknesses of their learning ability. Only a trained Educational Psychologist can administer an IQ test!

The WISC-III is divided into two distinct sections:

(a) The Verbal Section

(b) The Performance Section

The Verbal Section of the WISC-III IQ test

The Verbal Scale measures how well children are able to express themselves verbally and how well they are able to understand what is being said to them.

The sample questions in each section below are illustrative of the type of questions asked of people between the ages of 16 and 74. They are not the type of questions given to younger students!

VERBAL SCALE

The following six areas are tested to determine a person's verbal scale IQ.

1. Information

Task: Recall facts

Purpose: Establishes the amount of factual information acquired by the student in long-term memory – what people would describe as general knowledge. Such knowledge is dependent on school learning and accumulated life experience.

Examples: Who was Charles Darwin? What does the stomach do?

2. Vocabulary

Task: Explain the meaning of words

Purpose: To assess language development, knowledge and expression.
             Vocabulary is acquired through reading, school learning,
             environmental and cultural opportunity.

Examples: What is a *donkey?* What does *gamble* mean?

3. Comprehension

Task: Explain the meaning of concepts

Purpose: To assess commonsense, moral and social judgment.
             Comprehension is acquired through the development of
             conscience, moral sense and cultural influences.

Examples: Why are criminals locked up? Why should a promise be kept?

4. Similarities

Task: Finding common elements

Purpose: To examine categorical thinking, how things link together,
             abstract reasoning and verbal concept formation. These are
             skills are acquired through school learning, reading and
             general interest.

Example: In what way are a hat and a shirt alike?

5. Arithmetic

Task: Mental arithmetic

Purpose: To assess arithmetic reasoning and computational skill acquired through school learning and depending upon adequate attention span and concentration. How school based mathematics is related to real life situations.

Example: A workman earning 4 Euro per hour was paid 36 Euro. How long did he work?

6. Digit Span

Task: Remembering and repeating numbers

Purpose: To assess short-term memory which is dependent upon attention span and lack of distractibility.

Examples: Repeat the number 479

Repeat the number 43687

Repeat the number 15975

Repeat the number 486251378

(b) The Performance Section of the WISC-III IQ test

The Performance Scale measures the nonverbal areas of being able to perceive spatial relationships, such as putting puzzles together and being able to transfer visual information rapidly.

PERFORMANCE SCALE

The following six areas are tested to determine a person's performance level IQ.

1. Picture Arrangement

Task: Putting pictures in the correct order

Purpose: To assess ability to organise events in a sequence according to time and anticipate the outcome of a series of events. These skills would be acquired whilst reading comic strips and early reading books when many pictures are drawn to accompany the text.

Example: Arrange four or five given pictures in a story sequence as in a comic strip or storyboard.

2. Picture Completion

Task: Establish what is missing in a picture

Purpose: To measure the attention to detail when using visual memory. Visual memory is a major component used in retaining information in our long-term memory.

Example: Find the missing item in a picture e.g. a ladder without a rung.

3. Coding

Task: Copy a code

Purpose: To measure short-term visual memory, motor speed and accuracy. This is necessary when copying down words and numbers from the board in school.

Example: Copy the number 159837642

4. Block Design

Task: Make patterns with cubes

Purpose: To assess spatial visualization and the ability to see a pattern as a whole, rather than in sections. This also examines co-ordination of the hands and eyes.

Example: Use the blocks provided to reproduce a design as shown.

5. Object Assembly

Task: Assemble jigsaws

Purpose: To assess the person's ability to examine the jigsaw pieces of a picture, relate them to the picture and assemble as a complete picture. This requires visual perception and also hand eye co-ordination. These skills are acquired at an early age when playing with jigsaws etc.

Example: Assemble the pieces of a jigsaw puzzle forming a face or a car.

6. Mazes

Task: Follow a maze

Purpose: To measure the individual's ability to follow a visual pattern and to anticipate outcomes. Children playing with puzzle books at home or at school acquire these skills.

Example: Follow a maze by tracing along with a pencil.

In addition to Verbal and Performance IQ scores, the following abilities can also be measured:

Verbal Comprehension

Perceptual Organisation

Freedom from Distractibility

Perceptual Speed

Cross laterality: having mixed dominance between hand, foot, eye and ear. 45% of children with a Specific Learning Difficulty or dyslexia are cross lateral.

Directional Confusion: being unable to tell the difference between left and right without some mental aid such as remembering "I write with my right hand".

Free writing: the ability to write a short passage, which is age appropriate for the student.

Reading Speed: the number of words read in a suitable passage within one minute, which is compared to the average amount read by a student of a similar age.

Two-minute spelling: The student is asked to write down spellings called out and the number and accuracy of the spellings are compared with that of peers.

Nonsense passage: the student is asked to read a passage, which makes no sense. Some children are very good at guessing what words come next from the meaning of a passage. This test nullifies this and examines whether the student recognises each word or not.

These can prove very useful in determining an overall picture of a child's learning ability.

PLEASE NOTE:

There may well be a marked difference between the individual scores in the above tests. The Wechsler Scales provide scores for each of the subtests, so that the psychologist has a clearer picture of the individual's strengths and weaknesses.

It has been noted in the past that "practising" IQ tests may improve scores and thus affect the reliability of IQ tests. However, this will not increase the actual IQ of the individual and may prove detrimental to the child's long-term welfare as areas needing to be addressed may be overlooked!

The tests described above establish an individual's IQ and learning profile. Are there other tests to measure the educational achievement of an individual?

The following are tests that can be given to measure the knowledge and educational achievement at school and should be addressed as such. Not all Educational Psychologists will use all or any part of these tests as they regard the learning ability to be paramount rather than what has been learned to date.

A sample of some tests for educational achievement

WECHSLER DIMENSION TESTS

BRITISH ABILITY SCALE

ASTON INDEX

In addition to the WISC III there are a number of other related assessments, which focus on particular dimensions of learning. They include:

The Wechsler Objective Reading Dimensions (WORD)

Test reading (single word recognition and continuous prose)

Test spelling (sentence completion, dictation)

Test handwriting skills (sentence completion)

The Wechsler Objective Language Dimensions (WOLD)

Listening comprehension

Oral expression

Written expression

The Wechsler Objective Numeric Dimensions (WOND)

Mathematical reasoning

Numeric calculation

The scores attained in the WORD, WOLD and WOND are combined to give the Wechsler Individual Achievement Test (WIAT)

Conclusions and recommendations of the Educational Psychologist's report

This is perhaps the most important part of the Educational Psychologist's report and should address the individual needs of the child in a perfect educational world. However problems can arise because of the following:

Inadequate resources of the national education system of the country

Inadequate resources within the school the child attends

Large class sizes, which minimises the time for any individual instruction, which may be advised

Inadequate time allowance with a teacher trained in remedial education

The teacher may not have been trained to teach the programme recommended by the Educational Psychologist

There may be a distinct difference of opinion between the Educational Psychologist who observes the child on rare occasions and that of the teacher who sees the child on a daily basis

The practicality aspects of the recommendations in the Educational Psychologist's report.

What do I do with an Educational Psychologist's report?

An Educational Psychologist's report is extremely useful in the sense that the tests are standardised for all students and given by a person thoroughly trained in the administration and measurements of the results of the test.

The child's IQ can be assessed and appropriate expectation of academic achievement established for the child, parent, teacher and the school.

The strengths and weaknesses of the child's learning profile can be established and possibly addressed.

By referring to previous Educational Psychologist's reports it offers a long term indication of the student's progress and the benefits or otherwise of various recommendations from previous reports. It is for this reason that all reports should be kept in the order in which they were obtained.

All interested parties and future schools and educational establishments should be furnished with the report(s).

On examination of the Educational Psychologist's report(s) it is essential that an agreed "plan" and methodology is adopted by the parent, the teachers, the school, the educational psychologist and national examinations authorities for the maximum benefit of the **student.**

N.B. **Explain to the student, in terms they will understand, the results of the report and the implications and benefits of the future "plan" for him/her. If you do not discuss the report with the child then he/she will assume the worst. How would you feel if you underwent a test and the results were not discussed with you?**

Appendix 1. Details of terms and explanations that an educational Psychologist may use in a report.

Chapter 18

What causes dyslexia?

When speaking to students, parents, teachers, educational psychologists and school administrators the conversation usually includes this question. At the outset I would like to say there is no easy answer nor is there one answer but the hypotheses for the occurrence of dyslexia fall into three categories:

1. Biological aspects   dealing with genetics and neurology

2. Cognitive aspects   concerning how information is processed within the brain

3. Behavioural aspects   examining the role of learned behaviour and environment on dyslexia.

Before dealing with each of these headings there are two perspectives I would like the reader to consider:

Firstly, I think it is important to point out that very few people working in the field dyslexia even agree exactly on a rigid definition of dyslexia or its symptoms. Some people think it is purely a matter of spelling, reading and writing whereas others include other forms of behaviour for example time keeping, organisation and planning, sense of direction, knowing left and right etc. Those working in the field of dyslexia come from different backgrounds such as: individuals with dyslexia, parents of students with dyslexia, classroom teachers, teachers specialising in educational needs, educational psychologists, schools, school administrators, government policy makers and funding bodies. All of these individual groups have different agendas regarding possible solutions, training and finance.

There is no one structured provable theory for dyslexia that can predict future behaviour within fixed parameters for all individuals who have dyslexia, at the time of writing.

Secondly, statistical evidence often published in the general media can sometimes give an unbalanced viewpoint. For example, almost all studies show that the male brain is bigger than the female brain. The average brain of a male infant is between12-20% larger than that of a female infant. The head circumference of male infants is 2% larger than female infants; however, when we compare brain size relative to body weight there is almost no difference between males and females. Two infants who weigh the same, one male and one female, will have a similar size brain. In the same way the average brain weight in men is 11 to 12 per cent more than the average brain weight in women but again the average weight of men is considerably more than the average weight of women. Also absolute brain size has no link with level of intelligence! However can you imagine what the popular media could make of the above statistics? Statistics should always be interpreted within the parameters in which they are sourced and within the context in which they are applied as often a particular statistic or small group of statistics can be extracted and interpreted differently from the main body of work from where they are sourced!

Shaywitz's study in 1990 highlights how published statistics can often be skewed in nature. Traditional statistics regarding dyslexia were often school-based and more often than not these studies were identifying four times as many boys as girls exhibiting reading difficulties. The general public and, indeed many people working in the area of dyslexia, have long believed that dyslexia affected more boys than girls. More recent research found no significant difference in the prevalence of reading difficulties among boys and girls, when these studies were carried out, outside the school environment. This draws attention to the fact that the behavioural characteristics of boys in a classroom may have directed teachers' attention toward the academic difficulties of the boys more than the girls. (Shaywitz et al,1990).

Below is a brief summary of current opinions and their order does not signify any order of credibility:

1. Biological aspects

Biological theories can be addressed under two distinct headings:

(a) Genetic and (b) Neurological.

(a) Genetic:

Parents of children I work with in the field of dyslexia often ask "Did he get this problem from me?" "Am I responsible for her inability to read, because I had major problems reading when I was at school?" "Is it my genes?" and other such questions.

There is strong numeric evidence that dyslexia occurs in families, both immediate and extended, however this is not always so! (De Fries et al 1997). An individual may have dyslexia and yet sometimes there does not appear to be any occurrence of dyslexia within the family history. On the contrary, however, parents of children with dyslexia can often identify other members within their family, both present and past generations who had learning difficulties, within the realms of literacy.

Members of the general public tend to have a view that if a parent carries the gene for blue eyes then the gene is transmitted to the child who then may also have blue eyes. However, work has been carried out into the genetic profile of individuals with dyslexia and members of their family and studies seem to centre on chromosome 6 (Fisher et al 1999). It would nevertheless, be simplistic to take the view that a particular chromosome is responsible for the way in which a particular part of the brain is formed and hence for the way a person with dyslexia thinks, given the diversity of symptoms exhibited by a person with dyslexia.

For those working in the field of genetics, no individual gene has been proven to have a link with dyslexia; the method of transmission of dyslexia has yet to be formulated.

(b) Neurological:

In much the same way as particular parts of our body are used for different functions, such as using our hands to catch a ball, our ears to listen to music, our feet and legs to walk and our nose to smell, particular parts of our brain are used for different functions. Anatomy is the study of various sections of our body and neuro-anatomy is the study of different parts of the brain.

By carrying out autopsies on individuals who had dyslexia differences have been found between the brains of those people with dyslexia and those people who do not have dyslexia. Differences in the cerebellum, which is associated with phonological skills, have been reported by Fawcett et al (1999). The brains of people associated with dyslexia exhibit symmetry, the left and right hemispheres being of similar size, whereas the brains of people who do not exhibit dyslexia are, in general, asymmetric - the left hemisphere is larger than the right hemisphere. (Best and Demb, 1999).

Chapter 5 of the book is dedicated to eye tracking and as this has already been discussed it is only mentioned here. This is not to say that this aspect is unimportant as many people working in the field of dyslexia consider eye-tracking difficulties to be a cornerstone of reading difficulties. Many researchers have found that defects in the magno-cellular system between the eye and the part of the brain that processes visual information. The magno-cellular system, which deals with our ability to see moving images, is smaller in the brains of people with dyslexia. This makes reading harder because the brain has to quickly interpret the different letters and words which the eyes see as they scan words and sentences. These differences contribute towards our understanding of the differences in detecting motion and patterns, exhibited by individual with dyslexia while reading. (Geswind and Galaurda).

These are just a few examples of many studies yielding evidence that the physical brain has physical differences for people with dyslexia.

The studies cited above attempt to highlight the biological aspects, both genetic and neurological, that could result in individuals learning differently. Although a small number have been referred to, there are numerous other studies that explain certain aspects of dyslexia. Nevertheless, biological theories do not fully explain or embrace the notion of the malleability of the brain.

Imagine three children born into a family, identical triplets, each is born with two arms, two legs, a torso and a head. One child may grow up and their hobby is weight lifting, one child may develop an interest in tennis and the third child may develop an interest in chess. They would develop three different types of body from extremely muscular with slow reactions for the weight lifter, quick athletic reaction for the tennis player and a sedentary body for the chess player. Yet, each child is born with the same parents and, because they are identical triplets, each will have a very similar genetic profile. Environment, nutrition and behaviour have produced three very different bodies and, in the same way, the way each of us thinks has an effect on the way we develop our brain!

Scientists have demonstrated that animals reared in a comfortable and stimulating environment have more complex brains than those reared in a deprived background lacking stimulation. Using brain scanning techniques neuro-scientists have illustrated similar differences in development in a child's brain. Professor Bruce Perry studied brain scans of Romanian orphans exposed to severe neglect, which showed that the lack of stimulation resulted in poor development in the prefrontal cortex. Another example of the effects of stimulating the brain was carried out by Ypsilanti, Michigan. In a 30 year study, 123 severely socially-disadvantaged children, under 4 years of age, were exposed to a high quality, pre-school environment of stimulation with other children and adults. These same children were surveyed through to adulthood and it was found that they were less likely to depend on social services, and more likely to own their own home compared to their peers.

If at some stage in the future a gene can be shown to be responsible for either the biological or structural aspect of the brain of a person with dyslexia then it should be emphasised that the brain we are born with is malleable and can be developed by environment, emotional support and different learning methodologies.

2. Cognitive aspects

(a) Brain Processing:

Complex thinking processes, reading for an example, really should be considered as a multilevel function involving the interaction of many different parts of the brain. By using brain scans 30 years ago, it was possible to find what parts of the brain were working when performing a complex task such as reading. Brain scans have been developed to such an extent that not only can we discover what parts of the brain are working, but also, when and how they communicate and interlink with each other when performing such tasks as reading.

One example is given by Gabrieli and Klingberg of Stamford University who used diffusion tensor magnetic resonance imaging DTI to examine myelin sheaths which act as insulation of nerve cells in the brain. Two groups of people were selected; one group which had dyslexia and a second group which had not got dyslexia. Each individual was given a standardised reading test while his or her brain was being scanned. Results suggested that those individuals who had the best myelination scores in the temporo-parietal region which controls most language processing also have the best reading ability and vice versa. The efficiency of the interaction between various segments of the brain seems to be the determining factor.

A second example is the study by Richards of the University of Washington in Seattle using a form of MRI called echo-planar spectroscopic imaging (PEPSI). He monitored two groups, one had dyslexia, the other group had not. While carrying out a music test, no difference resulted. However, during the language tasks it was found that the students with dyslexia were using over four times as much area of the brain to carry out the language tasks as the group without dyslexia. This indicated that the brain was using more processing power for the students with dyslexia, which certainly dismisses the theory that people with dyslexia are in some ways "slow" when using their brain!

Chapter 4 referred to recent research being carried out by Dr. John Gabrieli and Dr. Torlel Klingberg at Stanford University highlighting difficulties with the speed at which the sound signals are transmitted along the nerve fibres within the auditory system. Individuals with phonetic difficulties exhibited slower passage of signals resulting in decreased ability to process the different sounds as they appear to crowd into each other. This problem may have a physical cause and it seems possible that inadequate myelin insulation of nerve fibres may be involved.

When two groups of adults, with and without dyslexia, were given a standardised reading test, DTI scans of their brains indicated that there was a difference between the two groups in the degree of myelination in the temporoparietal region of the brain's left hemisphere. This is the section of the brain that seems to control most language processing.

It is of course commonly known that, if a child suffers from frequent colds and throat infections in the first five years, the ears can become blocked which may result in impaired hearing. This condition is commonly known as "Glue Ear" and in medical terms "conductive hearing loss". Inserting tiny tubes or grommets in to the ear, which allows the fluid to drain off and hence improve hearing, mostly treats this condition. If this condition is not detected at an early stage, then a delay in phonetic awareness may result. Some members in the medical field estimate that 95% of children who have had grommets fitted between the ages of 4 and 7 will exhibit difficulties with processing of sound and may show symptoms of phonetic deafness.

(b) Sensory processing

People experience the world through the five senses seeing, hearing, touch, smell and taste. Most of us use one sense more than others and this becomes our dominant sense and it is reflected in our thinking processes and our language. In the main people are predominantly visual, auditory or kinaesthetic so let us examine the following three brief descriptions of a walk through a wood.

Visual description:

Rebecca was wearing a bright red woollen tweed coat and matching scarf as she walked through the woods, she looked up and watched the sunlight dancing on the golden autumn leaves creating an endlessly moving pattern on the path in front of her. As she looked along the grey gravel path she could see a small, whitewashed cottage in the distance. The grey smoke was curling from the chimney and spiralling upwards from the golden thatched roof. As she approached the olive green door she noticed it was slightly ajar. Using the ancient pitted brass knocker she knocked on the door three times without an answer. She walked inside to a gloomy red tiled kitchen with twisted smoked beams above and she noticed a black range on top of which was a copper saucepan. She lifted the lid and saw strawberry jam bubbling inside.

Auditory description:

As Rebecca was walking through the woods she could hear the wind rustling in the autumn leaves and creaking of the branches. She enjoyed listening to crunching of her feet on the gravel path. which led to the cottage. The jackdaws perched on the ridge of the thatched roof flapped their wings and cawed disapprovingly on her approach. The knocker on the front door made an inappropriately loud ringing noise has she tried to announce her arrival. As though was no answer from inside she pushed on the door, which creaked in protest on opening. She could hear a busy bubbling noise from the saucepan on the range and the lid of the saucepan danced with a metallic rhythm. Rebecca was very much aware of the loud clicking noise, which her shoes made when crossing the tiled floor. With a gentle clink she lifted the rid of the saucepan and the strawberry jam was busy bubbling inside as if to enthusiastically welcome her presence.

Kinaesthetic description:

Rebecca felt invigorated on a warm autumn day as she felt her feet crunching on the gravel path. Rebecca snuggled into her tweed scarf and she enjoyed the warmth it offered. She diverted continuously so that she could kick airily through the small wind blown heaps of dead leaves formed at either side of the path, the leaves yielded effortlessly to her kicks. As she approached the cottage she could feel the excitement forming in her tummy has she was one of the few people who knew of the existence of the cottage in the lonely woods. As she lifted the knocker on the door she remembered how heavy it felt in her hand as if the knocker itself did not wish to be disturbed. As she pushed on the heavy wooden door it resisted slightly but when she looked inside she remembered with fondness the welcoming warm cottage kitchen. The tiled kitchen floor felt firm under foot compared to the gravel path she had walked upon. On reaching for the handle of the saucepan she could feel the bubbling vibration of what was cooking inside. She lifted the heavy metal lid and she was delighted to see the strawberry jam cooking.

When reading the above three brief descriptions a visual reader will prefer the visual description, the auditory reader the auditory description and the same for the kinaesthetic reader. In general we prefer to read an author whose style of writing is similar to our style of thinking. Being visual, auditory or kinaesthetic is one aspect or characteristic of style of writing.

It is a matter of interest to teachers that teachers who are primarily visual will relate to an essay written in visual language more easily than an essay, which is written in either kinaesthetic or auditory language. In the same way an examiner who is auditory will relate to an auditory essay more easily than an essay that is written in primarily visual or kinaesthetic language. It is for this reason that teachers should explain to more mature students this difference and students in general should be taught to use descriptive language for visual auditory and kinaesthetic examiners.

Of course each of us can think in terms of visual, auditory or kinaesthetic and in terms of cocktail of two or all three modes of thinking but each of us has a primary or dominant mode of thinking. This mode of thinking expresses itself in our language when we communicate with each other. Read the following phrases and it is simple to identify whether the person is primarily visual, auditory or kinaesthetic:

"How or you feeling today?"

"You looking great today!"

"I hear you are in great form"

"I can understand what you are saying but it is only now I get the big picture"

"I feel it is a problem but I know I can get to grips with it"

"The main speaker explained it so well that now all clicks into place"

Predicate:

This word is formed from two parts "pre" from the Latin meaning before and dictate from the Latin verb "dicio" meaning to speak. So predicates are words or phrases that tell us which part of the brain visual, auditory or kinaesthetic the speaker or writer is using when they express themselves.

Conversely if you are speaking to a child, or telling a story to a child, and you use language that is visually based then that child will respond by using the visual part of his brain to understand what you are saying. Similarly if you are using auditory or kinaesthetic language then that child will also use those parts of the brain to process and understand what is being talked about.

In summary if a child has a parent, guardian, sibling, friend or teacher who is a dominant personality for that child and that dominant personality uses visual predicates in their language then that child will use visual processing in his brain. He will also use visual predicates in his language to express answers to questions he is being asked. This is an example of how we can use our conscious mind to use language but at an unconscious level we learn how to use our brain by virtue of the predicates of the language we use.

This hypothesis clearly supports our model of how some students have difficulty in learning spellings, as outlined in Chapter 4. If a student is predominantly an auditory or kinaesthetic processor and that same student has trouble in accessing their visual memory, this may explain why it may be difficult for that student to naturally progress from a phonetic method to a visual strategy for learning spellings. Similarly, these same students may exhibit difficulties in comprehension while reading (Chapter 6), essay writing difficulties (Chapter 7), and/or may present sequencing or organisational difficulties, and/or have a poor sense of time awareness (Chapter 8) as represented by the dyslexia@bay™ model of the brain (Chapter 16). By "switching on" their visual memory, these students can learn how to process visually, and many of these characteristics can be alleviated.

This field of research holds great possibilities for the future. If we could profile how the individual person with dyslexia exhibits the symptoms of dyslexia by identifying the individual areas of the brain do not communicate efficiently, we could understand the cause of the symptoms. Then perhaps we could design teaching methods specifically to suit the neurological profile of each student with dyslexia.

3. Behavioural aspects

We have all learned behaviour from our parents, siblings and others in our everyday environment as infants and young children. Some of this behaviour is learned at an unconscious level and some of it is learned at a conscious level and some is learned at the crossover between conscious and unconscious learning.

When a baby is lying in a crib it cries when it is hungry or uncomfortable and this is a behaviour that is stimulated by a physical need. As the baby grows the baby starts to smile. This behaviour of smiling is not a response to a physical need - in fact the baby learns to mimic the behaviour of others. As adults look at the baby and smile, then the baby imitates the behaviour and starts to smile itself. Of course, the baby learns that when it smiles it gets cuddled and given attention. It does not take long for the baby to learn to smile and stimulate affectionate behaviour towards it. The initial learning of the behaviour was at an unconscious level but once this skill has been learned and practised at a conscious level then the baby learns to affect the behaviour of others. Just watch any baby and how they can influence the behaviour of the parents!

A child learning to read may learn to run their finger underneath the line as they are reading if a parent or sibling reads with that characteristic. Sometimes this may have a negative influence on a child's reading ability. A child may learn to hold a book at a certain angle by mimicking a parent or sibling. A child may learn to hold his head at a particular angle when reading because he has seen an older person hold their head at a particular angle when reading. This angle may indeed inhibit fluent reading by the child. These are just a few characteristics and behaviours a child may learn at an unconscious level when reading. These behaviours may, or may not, be aiding the child's ability to read.

A chef or wine taster during training will learn to discriminate tastes to a higher degree than is considered normal. Similarly a blind child who is taught to read Braille will learn to discern touch to such a degree that he is to be able to read quite fluently by using touch alone. A musician has been trained to have a musical ear and we can think of many other occupations in which the different senses have been trained to perceive at a level well above the norm.

Some people who work in the field of dyslexia believe that behaviour is learned along the whole spectrum from unconscious learning to conscious learning, and all points in between. They believe that effective reading behaviour is a behaviour that can be learned and vice versa that reading difficulties are behaviours that can be learned. This is why they believe that dyslexia can occur in families.

Learning to read and choice of reading material can also be learned at a conscious level. If the parents in a family read on an ongoing basis within the home, then the young child will observe this behaviour.

Social learning theorists have shown that children can learn vicariously, which is evident in their mimicking of the behaviour of the parents or other role models. For example, holding up the telephone and having long imaginary conversations and very often about the same subject as the parent has just spoken about on the telephone. Children in this way e.g. washing dishes, brushing floors, using a hose in the garden, pulling at the steering wheel of the car etc, pick up lots of behaviour patterns.

Equally, it is important to note that attitudes are all learned through social interaction, which is frequently happens vicariously too!

It is not uncommon for a preschool infant to hold up a book or magazine, that a parent has just read, and then pretend to read as the parent has just done. In this manner the child can be made aware that reading is an everyday occurrence within the home. Conversely the opposite is also true, if it is not common for the infant to observe adults and older siblings reading, then there is no reading behaviour to mimic!

The television programmes watched by parents will have an effect upon the television programmes chosen by children within the home. If one or other parents watch television "soaps" then that may well be the choice subsequently of the children of that home. If natural history programmes are watched within the home then that will be the choice of the children. The same may be taken for documentaries, drama, the news, current affairs programmes and films of various types.

This choice of reading material within the home also has an affect upon the reading material selected by the student. If newspapers and magazines are selected by both parents and other adults in the home then the value of reading that material may be transferred to the student. If one or other parents read novels of a certain category then this also will affect the choice of reading material of the student.

The atmosphere created by the parent when reading also has an affect upon the child. Some adults read a novel when the room is quite quiet, whereas others read with music playing the background, others may read only in bed before going to sleep, others may read the newspaper while eating breakfast, others may read the newspaper while watching television. These are examples of several different atmospheres, some preferred by some and others, which could not be tolerated by some.

Where, when and in which atmosphere reading takes place by parents in the home has a direct bearing on the value of reading and the reading material of children of that particular home.We may unconsciously create ceremonies within family life that pertain to reading. In my own home on Sunday morning after breakfast the family went to the local shop where Sunday newspapers, children's comics and each individual's favoured sweets were bought. On returning home the family sat in the sitting room with music playing in the background each enjoying their own favourite sweets whilst reading. This was always a ceremony before whatever other family activity occurred on Sundays. This was not a ceremony that was thought out - it just evolved but to this day each member of the family, now all adults, perform the same ceremony. In the same fashion each member of the family still reads in bed before going sleep, again a habit picked up from reading stories to the children just before they went to sleep when they were very young.

Demonstration:

Close your eyes and for a moment remember when you saw your parents reading when you were young. Remember where and when you saw them reading and what sort of reading material they read. Ask yourself now what reading behaviour you have inherited from them and what sort of reading behaviour you would want your children to inherit from you.

Consideration of the effects of our role models in the development of our attitudes and behaviour plays a part not necessarily in explaining the causes of dyslexia, but in how dyslexia can be exacerbated. If a child has persistent reading/spelling or writing problems, and has been brought up in an environment where such activities are not valued, the child may not attempt to practise these activities sufficiently in order to overcome the difficulties.

This attitude may be reinforced by one or both parents, disparaging any attempt on the child's behalf to overcome his difficulty, by overtly or covertly expressing their attitude towards the futility of reading/writing or spelling. How often have we heard adults utter, in the presence of their child, "I was always a poor reader/speller/writer and I managed to get along fine without it!"? The child may then reach a state of learned helplessness, in which he or she becomes apathetic about trying the activity.

Similarly, such effects will explain the fact that many students with dyslexia can have low self-esteem. Once learned helplessness has set in students who are conscious of their difficulties, compared to the abilities of their peers, may develop a poor self-image. Consequently, the avoidance of the activities will result in a self-fulfilling prophecy, with a low-self esteem ensuing!

If there are so many theories about the cause of dyslexia which one is true?

It is quite confusing for a parent or teacher entering the world of dyslexia for the first time to find that there has been so much research in the field of dyslexia which has led to many different theories as to the cause of dyslexia. We expect in the world of science using such sophisticated instruments such as brain scanning equipment, identifying genetic profiles etc. that we would have the answer by now instead of a wide spectrum of theories some of which are mentioned above.

It is my own personal belief that all the above theories have a degree of relevance and this is because of the variety of characteristics exhibited by different people with dyslexia. I have dealt with people with dyslexia from five years of age to eighty-two years of age from 10 different countries and over a period of over 20 years and I have yet to meet two people with dyslexia who are the same! Is it any surprise then that all of the above theories have relevance in their own right?

Let us examine three individuals I have worked with:

Mary:

Mary was nine years of age when we first met. Mary did not enjoy school and particularly detested Fridays. She was a rather clumsy child and extremely anxious insisting on sitting beside her mother. She told me she could not read and had absolutely no interest in learning to read. Mary's parents noted that when she did read sometimes she covered her left eye with the palm of her left hand. After a visit to the optician her sight was declared perfectly normal. She had few friends in school and felt she was not as good as the rest of her peers in the classroom and certainly did not enjoy the sports field.

Mary's problem was that on Fridays they had a spelling test, which consisted of writing down the spellings that they were supposed to have learned during the week. Her teacher was very sympathetic to her case and never asked Mary to read out loud either in class or in a small group. She reduced the amount of spellings required for Mary to learn each night compared to the rest of the class. She and other students in the class were given "special spellings" which consisted of 3, 4, or 5 letter words. Her parents worked diligently through a phonics programme given by the school to help her learn these spellings but with minimal results.

Furthermore, as Mary could not remember her spellings she could not recognise the spellings when she came across them in reading material.

Mary read with one eye only, voluntary occlusion, because at close distances her eyes were not working together. Mary had discovered that she could "see the page better" using only one eye. She certainly did not make any pictures in her head of what she could read and therefore had little or no comprehension. Mary also had major difficulty remembering her tables and often got the wrong answer in her sums having decided she was very bad at sums.

When Mary was a baby she did not crawl but "bottom shuffled". She had a history of messy eating when young preferring to use her hands. She had not been able to learn to skip and took a much longer time that normal to learn to ride a bicycle. Her ability to catch a ball especially one thrown at head height was negligible. She felt useless at games and thus did not take part in them. Hence the cycle of not playing games meant she did not improve and because she did not improve she did not want to practice the games.

The result of the above was not Mary had little or no interest in school, understandably so, and suffered from a low sense of self-esteem.

Mary's programme:

As the phonics programme had not worked with Mary it was decided to train Mary in a visually based programme instead. Mary's short-term auditory memory was limited so she was taught to see words rather than hear words. Once trained in these skills Mary was able to remember her spellings. Mary was given the list of the 100 most common words and later Mary was given the Dolch basic sight vocabulary list of two hundred and twenty words that are "service words" (verbs, adjectives, pro nouns, adverbs, prepositions, conjunctions) which can be learned through the use of pictures. By learning these lists Mary was then able to recognise 75 per cent of the words used in schoolbooks, library books, comics, magazines and newspapers. It was important to point out to Mary that this was the complete list of words she was required to visualise. Mary was quite surprised how many of the words she already knew. These lists are given in the appendix 2. After visualising her lists of words and being able to recognise them Mary was given a page to read and her first task was to take a yellow highlighter and mark all the words she could recognise. Next she was asked to read the page with only the highlighted word and ignore the rest and then she asked what was the story about. She was pleasantly surprised that she could understand the page even though she had left out lots of words! Mary at this point had a new concept of what reading was all about with the result that Mary was very keen to learn longer and longer spellings. One of her favourite childhood films was Mary Poppins. She became so adept at spelling long words that her party piece was to be able to spell "supercalifragilisticexpialidocious" after a particular song in the movie. On being able to spell this word and remember it she wrote to me to say she was no longer a bad speller but a "super speller" instead.

Mary was given distinct eye exercises such that she would be able to read with two eyes and with this skill and the fact that she could remember all her spellings from the Dolch list and 100 most used words her mechanical reading improved dramatically.

Subsequent to this Mary was also taught how to make pictures in her head of the material she was reading and this introduced a huge new element into what Mary's understanding of what reading was all about.

As regards her tables, Mary had found it very difficult to remember nursery rhymes so it was not really surprising that she found it difficult to remember her tables. Instead Mary was given a visual strategy for remembering her tables, which she found much easier and she thought possible.

Mary was also given a series of cross lateral exercises and other physical exercises which are made much more easy by virtue of the fact that she had been taught how to use her two eyes in unison. Once she had managed to perform these exercises comfortably, she was then encouraged to perform them to music hence promoting a sense of rhythm within her body. She was encouraged to swim as, in this particular exercise, the water maintained her body in balance and the she did not have to learn to keep her own balance.

Mary's result:

Mary became keen on swimming and then was amazed how easy it was to learn to skip and naturally ball skills and other more sophisticated games followed. Mary never became a gifted sports person, however her skills did improve to such a degree that she did enjoy sports as long as they were non-contact sports. She learned to enjoy reading and has become very particular in her choice of reading material, which she insists in selecting for herself. She now looks forward with anticipation to her Friday spelling test as she now feels that she can "show off" her spellings skills. Mary's opinion of her ability to do sums changed totally when after learning her tables she was able to get "the right answer". Mary is now a very happy young lady. She enjoys dancing immensely and attends school with an ever-increasing sense of self-esteem.

Peter:

Peter was aged 16, of a typical physical build and with a cheerful personality. He had above average ability at mathematics and science. He scored well in school exams in maths, applied mathematics, physics and chemistry. When answering questions on test papers in physics and chemistry he chose the mathematical type of question. He had been diagnosed as having dyslexia in his middle years of primary school and had had to deal with difficulty in learning to spell and also remembering his spellings. He knew that, if he answered a descriptive question in an exam, he would make a lot of spelling mistakes and so he avoided this type of question. Even though he had a keen interest in biology he chose not to study it because he felt his spelling difficulties would affect his results and ultimately his choice of course at university.

Peter complained that after reading for more than 25 or 30 minutes his eyes felt tired and he would have to take a break. He was also aware that others in his class could read material once and have full comprehension of the material, whereas he had to read the same material two or three times. This confused him, as he knew he was at least as clever as his peers.

Peter took part in all school sports activities and excelled at middle distance running. He enjoyed school and being with his friends and the only blot on landscape was the English class.

Peter's problem:

He enjoyed the poetry, novels and plays but felt "his dyslexia" would prevent him from passing the English exams with even the minimum of marks. He needed a pass in English for entry to university despite his well above average ability at science subjects. He was keen to solve his problems so that he could go to university to study engineering.

Peter's programme:

Peter's "tired eyes" were due to an eye-tracking problem, which could be resolved by suitable exercises. He was made aware that his eye-tracking problem had been making reading more difficult for him and that his eye-tracking problem would be solved within a short period of time by carrying out the suggested exercises.

It was explained to him that he had not been making any type of visual representation in his head of the material he had been reading. He was given a mental skills programme to enable him to make visual constructions in his head in order to more easily comprehend what was being read. Peter was also taught how to make notes using diagrams, symbols and colours as well as words to represent his thoughts on paper, which could be easily understood and revised in a minimum amount of time.

As regards spellings Peter was found to be phonetically deaf. Once this was explained to him, he adopted a visual strategy for learning his spellings, which not only made spellings easier to learn in the first place but also solved the problem of forgetting his spellings.

Peter's result:

Peter was a keen student and he wanted to solve his problem. He practised his eye exercises and mental skills programme with diligence. Peter went on to study engineering at university no longer complaining of tired eyes. He could read and concentrate for longer periods of time, had a structured study programme and thoroughly enjoyed a full social life.

Michael

Michael was 67 years of age when he came to see me. He explained to me that he left school when he was 11 years of age and that school had been a nightmare for him. His father wanted him to help him on the farm rather than to bother wasting his time at school. He told his son school had never been any good for him and he learned more by working in the fields. Michael was very good with his hands and, after serving his time as a carpenter; he found he enjoyed working with wooden boats. He had a very successful business repairing old wooden boats and his business just grew and grew. I could tell by the expression on his face that he thoroughly enjoyed, and was proud of, his work and the flourishing boatyard. He had been a keen sportsman in his youth and was now a very proficient low handicap golfer His business was very successful and he was considered "very well off". I had worked with his eight year-old grandson and not only had grandson and parents enjoy the results but also his grandfather Michael. Michael was very proud when his grandson sat on his knee reading him a story. Michael had managed not only to keep his dyslexia a secret from his grandson but also from the child's father who was his son. He had several people working in his business none of whom were aware that he could neither read nor write. His wife attended to the office and was responsible for all administration for the business.

I wondered at the time why Michael had come to me at this age, as he was a very happy family man and successful businessman who had not let dyslexia interfere with his attitude for a successful life. I asked Michael why he felt he should come to see me, as dyslexia had not seemed to be a problem to him. I am a great believer in the phrase "if it ain't broke don't fix it". Lots of adults ask me when socialising whether I think they should address their dyslexia and I always reply that if it is not getting in their way then why bother. I then recount cases of people with severe problems resulting from dyslexia and they realise that having dyslexia and considering oneself "dyslexic" are two different things. This may seem strange from someone working in the field of dyslexia however there is no one on this planet that is perfect in every way. I know a lot of golfers who have problems with their legs but still play a mean game of golf. I know people who have had severe automobile accidents but by driving a suitably altered car they drive around on a daily basis. I know adults who have difficulty with numbers and sums but it only became a problem when they started to do homework with the children. My advice is the children will grow up, the homework will disappear and so will your problem.

Michael's problem:

Michael had a similar problem with dyslexia as a lot of adults. He knew that at the age of 67 he would not be able to physically work a full day forever. He felt particularly that on winter days he would be unable to fill his time on retirement. I asked him whether it would be important to be able to write, to which he replied 'No, it is only important that I can read'. I then asked what sort of articles he would like to read and he replied the newspaper. In addition, as he was interested in boats he would like to be able to read books about sea journeys particularly long, single-handed sailing voyages.

Michael had no eye problems other than long sight, which was perfectly normal for an adult of his age. He did note that when young the words and letters seemed to move about the page but that that had stopped as he had become older. I find this quite common among adults who seek help. He had attended some literacy classes, which started with sounding off letters and small words, which he did not find beneficial and he found the classes very tiresome.

Michael's programme:

I knew Michael had a very well developed visual memory as he had to be able to read plans of boats and remember them to carry out his work. I encouraged him to cut out words from groceries and drinks packages and various commodities somewhere in a workshop. I also asked that he cut out words from invoices sent to him from suppliers of his business that he would be familiar with. By teaching him various techniques of visualisation with familiar words we were able very easily get him to read first of all sentences and then paragraphs. As he was familiar with all the words, as well as the contents of the packets it was easy for him to make pictures in his mind of the sentences that he was reading. I encouraged him to read the invoices of the business to try to make pictures of the materials that the company had ordered. Within two weeks not only was he able to do this quite easily he became quite agitated to find companies were sending him materials that he had not even asked for and charging them to his account. He immediately grasped the benefits of him being able to read! He then insisted on writing down the list of various materials for the boatyard and insisted on giving them personally to the suppliers.

I asked him how he had learnt to write so easily and he replied that he did not have to write in sentences but just single words and figures. So he just imagined seeing the word written on the packets in his head and pretended his fingers and pen were a chisel just etching out the words on the paper! He was very surprised when I expressed total amazement at not only his ability to write but also the speed with which he had learned to write.

We repeated the same procedure for all different parts of boats and I encouraged him to look at the Internet, which he enjoyed thoroughly. After a very short period of time he was able to down load articles about various sea voyages and read them, at which point he was amazed to find that this reading was "dead easy". It was not long before Michael read his first book of a sea voyage. Michael now has a vast number of books concerning voyages and has started to read fictional novels concerning the sea.

Conclusion:

As you can see each of these three cases presented with different problems, some with eye-tracking problems others not, some with poor visual memory others not, some with physical clumsiness others not, some with short-term memory problems others not etc. I hope you can also see that all of the theories mentioned earlier in this section come into play for each individual but to different degrees of importance. Having dealt with so many different individuals from different cultures and countries it is not hard to believe that dyslexia is caused by a cocktail of eye tracking and other biological causes, cognitive thinking processes and either learned or unlearned behaviour patterns.

The reader may feel frustrated having read this chapter expecting to find a fixed reason why dyslexia exists but I hope you may have an appreciation of the causes of dyslexia.

One final note, Michael wrote me a very interesting letter outlining how he was enjoying his semi-retirement and from his fireside chair he was able to explore every continent in the world and visit every period of time in history............. all by being able to read a book!

Chapter 19

Famous people who are reported to have/had dyslexia

We often hear of famous people who have coped with dyslexia and been successful in life. We are encouraged to tell our children about these people but who are/were they?

The following is a list of famous people, current and from the past, who, according to press reports, have/had dyslexia or have/had symptoms of dyslexia or related reading, spelling and writing difficulties. Some people from history who exhibited classic signs of dyslexia e.g. Leonardo da Vinci is also included. There are many other famous names that can be sourced on the Internet.

Architects
Lord Richard Rogers (Lloyd's Building, Pompidou Centre)
Jorn Utzon (Sydney Opera House)

Artists/Sculptors

Leonardo da Vinci   Andy Warhol

Pablo Picasso   Peter Scott

Auguste Rodin

Authors

Hans Christian Andersen	Ernest Hemingway
Agatha Christie	Roald Dahl
W.B. Yeats	Mark Twain
Lewis Carroll	

Actors/Entertainers

Harrison Ford	Robin Williams
Tom Cruise	Anthony Hopkins
Danny Glover	Bob Hoskins
Jack Nicholson	Steve McQueen
Whoppi Goldberg	George Burns
Susan Hampshire	Jeremy Irons
Dustin Hoffman	Eddie Izzard
Oliver Reed	Felicity Kendall
Ben Elton	Marlon Brando
Billy Bob Thornton	Sarah Miles

Computers

Steve Jobs (Apple) Computers	Mike Norris (Computacenter)
William Hewlett (Hewlett Packard)	John Chambers (Cisco)

Entrepreneur

Anita Roddick (Body Shop)   Charles Schwab (Investor)

Richard Branson (Virgin)   Ted Turner (Turner Broadcasting Systems)

Alan Sugar (Amstrad)   F.W. Woolworth (Woolworths)

Henry Ford (Ford)   Lord McAlpine

Paul Orfalea (Kinkos)

Fashion

Tommy Hilfiger

Jodie Kidd

Leaders

Winston Churchill   Thomas Jefferson

George Washington   Nelson Rockerfeller

Michael Heseltine   Woodrow Wilson

John F. Kennedy

Music

John Lennon   Liam Gallagher

Mozart   Enrico Caruso

Beethoven   Nigel Kennedy

Military

General George S. Patton

Thomas Jonathan "Stonewall" Jackson

Film Makers/Photographers

Steven Speilberg   David Bailey

Walt Disney   Ansel Adams

Scientists and Inventors

Albert Einstein   Charles Darwin

Thomas Edison   Werner Von Braun

Michael Faraday   Wright Brothers

Alexander Graham Bell   Louis Pasteur

Sports People

Dennis Bergkamp (Footballer)   Steven Redgrave (Rowing)

Paul Merson (Footballer)   Muhammad Ali (Boxing)

Duncan Goodhew (Swimmer)   Magic Johnson (Basketball)

Johnny Herbert (Motor racing)   Diamond Dallas Page (Wrestling)

Jackie Stewart (Motor racing)   Chris Boardman (Cyclist)

Sandy Lyle (Golfer)   Carl Lewis (Athlete)

Chapter 20

Learning differences and disabilities

A number of students in the classroom have difficulties with spelling and reading which are due to dyslexia but there are others whose learning difficulties are due to other factors. Having conducted many workshops for teachers in schools, I have listened to teachers who have students in their classroom who have been diagnosed and labelled but the teachers are unaware of what these labels mean. Below is a brief summary of some other learning difficulties experienced in the classroom.

In Chapter 2, I briefly introduced the topic of learning differences, embracing the notion that dyslexia should be viewed as a learning difference rather than a learning difficulty. In this Chapter I will draw a further distinction between learning differences and learning disabilities.

There is considerable variation on policy between the terminologies used in statements worldwide, in defining types of learning difficulties. However, for the purpose of this book I refer to two categories of learning difficulties:

Learning Differences

Learning Disabilities

(a) Learning Differences

This term refers to a disorder in one or more of the basic psychological processes, which affects the understanding or use of spoken or written language and/or the ability to listen, think, speak, write, spell or do numerical manipulations.

Learning Differences is an inclusive term that points to the fact that many children within educational systems who are experiencing difficulties within the normal school environment are often not identified for special education requirements. In Ireland, for example, the National Assessment of Reading Achievement in 1998 estimated that 10% of students in fifth class had serious literacy problems. In a present pilot scheme using 31 schools it was found that up to 20% of students were having learning differences.

Early diagnosis and intervention help to reduce the effect of learning differences so knowledge and identification of symptoms is essential for both parents and teachers alike. Whereas identification and help is quite common for dyslexia in the education system today there are other learning differences, which are less well recognised and addressed.

This spectrum of learning differences ranges from mild and short-term to severe and long-term. It is generally accepted that four times as many males as females have learning differences and that somewhere between 8 and 20% of students overall seem to have learning differences i.e. children who seem to experience difficulties with basic school subjects which are not commensurate with their age and level of intelligence. These educational difficulties occur despite normal school attendance record, environment, parental support and education opportunity.

So far in this book, the focus of learning differences has been on dyslexia. The following is a brief guide to other learning differences that may result in a student being incapable of coping in a normal school environment. These differences may or may not be accompanied by dyslexia.

ADD/ADHD

Dyscalculia

Dysgraphia

Dyspraxia

Developmental Speech and Language Disorders

Attention deficit disorder (ADD)/attention deficit hyperactive disorder (ADHD):

Children with attention deficit disorder easily become distracted and are unable to focus on a task for more than a very short period of time. They are unable to sit still for very long and indulge in endless conversation. They are distracted in a classroom environment by any movement by any other student. These children seem unable to follow a simple set of instructions to complete a task and may be impulsive by nature. They tend to be poor at mathematics as they are unable to concentrate for any length of time or follow a sequence of instructions. A student with attention deficit disorder is often poorly organised and often forgets books, sports equipment and clothing when going to and from school. These students may be of average intelligence but do not make the progress of their peers due to a lack of attention to school work in general and a tendency to put things off. If the student is also hyperactive, with the above symptoms then the term attention deficit hyperactive disorder ADHD may be used.

Dyscalculia:

Students who have dyscalculia can exhibit a range of difficulties in mathematics. Some may have difficulties in basic operations, which involve short-term memory for example, addition, subtraction, multiplication and division and in the recognition of their corresponding symbols. Other students may have difficulty in understanding the language of mathematics or abstract concepts. Memory of facts, formulae and sequential tasks can be difficult too. As I referred to in Chapter 8 many people with dyslexia have difficulties with sequential and logical tasks. This can obviously have a negative effect one's ability to do mathematical problems.

Dysgraphia:

Dysgraphia can be evident in a student's actual gross and fine motor co-ordination difficulties when writing.

Also characteristic are difficulties with spelling and the formulation of written essays or stories.

Dyspraxia:

Other names used are clumsy child syndrome, developmental co-ordination disorder (DCD), perceptuo-motor dysfunction, motor learning difficulties or minimal brain dysfunction. Experts in this field claim that as many as 6% of schoolchildren may in fact have dyspraxia.

Praxis is a Greek word that describes the ability to plan and co-ordinate a sequence of movements. Dys is a Greek prefix for bad. Parents often become aware of the situation when the child starts school. The teacher and parent who have older children who have progressed normally at school usually notice handwriting difficulties. The child will often become frustrated and as a result "won't sit still". These children will not be good at jigsaws, building blocks or at any constructional toy. Below is a list of activities where their skills may be noticeably different from their peers:

Throwing and catching a ball

Balancing and riding a bicycle

Jumpin

Holding a pencil

Hopping on one foot

Running and flapping the arms like a bird flaps its wings

Any cross lateral movement will cause confusion. (Moving a hand or foot across the midline that runs vertically from a spot between the eyes to a spot between the feet when standing.) A student with dyspraxia will be late to develop a mature grasp. They may also not judge distance accurately and hence jump off walls and railings, which are "too high" and result in injury. If there is a history of this then the child will become over protective of him/herself.

As a result of these difficulties a child soon becomes aware of his limitations with respect to his peers and tends not to practise these skills so he does not improve as his classmates do. The child will have difficulty playing sports, especially contact sports with the resulting social isolation and poor self-esteem as regards sports.

Some students with dyslexia also exhibit symptoms of dyspraxia. However, others are wonderfully well coordinated and are very good at sport.

Developmental speech and language disorders

Speech and language problems are often the earliest indicators of a learning difference. Students with developmental speech and language disorders may have difficulties producing speech sounds and/or in controlling their rate of speech (Articulation Disorder). Others may have difficulty in using spoken language to communicate or express themselves (Expressive Language Disorder), while some have trouble in understanding what other people say (Receptive Language Disorder)

(b) Learning Disabilities

This term refers to a neurological disorder, which affects how a person receives, processes or expresses information, which can have an impact on the ability to acquire basic academic skills.

Autism

Asperger syndrome

Down syndrome

Fragile X syndrome

Turner syndrome

Autism:

An Australian psychiatrist Leo Kanner described a type of learning disorder that begins at birth or within the first three years of life. For many years the incidence of autism was about 5 in 10,000 live births, however since the early 1990s rates as high as 60 in 10,000 have been reported worldwide.

Individuals with autism are perfectly normal in appearance but can exhibit behaviour that is markedly different from the range of normal behaviour.

Characteristics include:

Difficulty in developing reciprocal relationships with people

Difficulty in communicating verbally and non-verbally with people

Difficulty in adjusting their repertoire of behaviour to varying circumstances

Tantrum throwing

Repetitive activities with no apparent purpose

Obsessive desire for routine activities and sameness

Children with autism often have accompanying syndromes, for example epilepsy and Fragile X syndrome.

Asperger syndrome:

Asperger syndrome has similar symptoms to autism. However the Austrian, Hans Asperger, noted that the child is not as severely affected and he noticed, that this disorder is much more common than autism. Yet, it is still a very rare condition and few people, even professionals, know much about it and often have little experience of it. Asperger syndrome seems to affect more boys than girls.

It is characterised by the following:

Extremely poor social skills

Little or limited ability to form friendships, due to the lack of empathy which the student should feel with his peers

Clumsy and un-coordinated movements

Body language and postures coupled with limited facial expression give rise to poor social interaction.

Children with Asperger syndrome are often loners in school and they do not enjoy team activity. This situation may become more acute when the child is in second level education. A doctrinaire attitude may give an impression of superior ability but this is usually not accompanied by actual ability. The fascination for small everyday objects and the desire for sameness of a child with Autism is reflected in a child with Asperger syndrome as an intense absorption in objects which are categorised as the same but are different e.g., knowing all about cars. They may well be very able at mathematics and hence become very good at engineering or science but with the total disregard of other areas.

Down syndrome

A British doctor John Langdon Down identified the condition in 1866 however the actual chromosomal nature of Down syndrome was not documented until 1959 by Levan and Tio who requested the name be changed from mongolism to Down syndrome. The incidence of Down syndrome has been variously reported as 1 in 800 live births to 1 in 1,100 live births. Down syndrome is due to an extra 21st chromosome, which causes an extra dose of some proteins. There are three types of Down syndrome Trisomy 21 (95%), Translocation (3-4%) and Mosaicism (1-2%). The average life expectancy for people with Down syndrome has increased from 2-3 years in 1920 to 57 today.

Every child with Down syndrome is different and abilities, level of learning, temperaments and interests all differ. These students may be able to learn well in a "normal" educational environment. The educational policy in most countries has been the integration of children with Down syndrome into ordinary schools rather than segregation in specialist schools where possible. A teaching assistant is generally required to support the child for at least part of the week. Some parents with a child with Down syndrome favour integration. They wish their child to be educated locally for social, transport and time considerations. These parents also cite the need for their child to have role models of children without special needs. For other parents a special school is the first choice. They feel that the child should be taught in a more specialised and protected environment with extra resources. The parents' wishes should be respected at all times and it is extremely important that more regular updates on children with Down syndrome are given to the parents.

The educational policy of the educational establishment attended by the child with Down syndrome may very greatly. At those schools where integration has been most successful teachers continuously remark on the very positive attitudes of the other students in the school and the benefits to the other children.

Fragile X syndrome:

Fragile X syndrome is a commonly inherited form of mental retardation caused by a fragile site or gap at the end of the long arm of the X-chromosome. It affects 1 in 1000 males and one in seven hundred and fifty females. For males the features are long and/or protruding ears, prominent jaw or long face and prominent forehead. There are no physical characteristics for females and the gene is carried through the female line.

These students often have recurrent ear infections and exhibit autism-like behaviour such as gaze aversion, preoccupation with objects, hand flapping and biting.

Intellectual disability occurs in approximately 80% of males and up to 50% of females and there may be speech delay. Learning difficulties may be subtle.

Fragile X syndrome children have strong functional life skills. They have strong imitation skills and will benefit greatly from being paired with a "buddy". These children work best with visual methods, whole word, number and pattern recognition preferably associated with a picture. Auditory sequencing should be avoided when learning. These students have poor auditory short-term memory. They will not make progress learning to read by a phonic methodology. Bright light should be avoided in the classroom situation, as they are sensitive to bright light.

Turner syndrome:

This chromosome abnormality identified by Dr. Henry Turner, which affects girls only (1:2000 live female births), may be physically diagnosed by a short stature, heavy neck skin and folds. These students may have the following characteristics: puffy hands and feet, droopy eyelids, low hairline, low-set ears and a broad chest. Students with Turner syndrome can be hyperlexic, which is they are usually excellent mechanical readers but will not comprehend what they have read. They have difficulty solving problems and have difficulty with spatial organisation and will learn spellings by rote. Students with Turner syndrome have learning difficulties/spatial awareness problems but not mental retardation.

Bibliography

Carter, R., *Mapping the Mind.* London: Whurr.

Chase, C., Rosen, G., and Sherman, G., *Developmental Dyslexia: Neural, Cognitive and Genetic Mechanisms.* Baltimore: York Press.

Gerber, A., *Language-Related Learning Disabilities: Their Nature and Treatment.* Baltimore: Brooks.

Heaton, P., and Winterson, P., *Dealing with Dyslexia.* London: Whurr.

Hulme, C., and Snowling, M., *Dyslexia: Biology, Cognition and Intervention.* London: Whurr.

Marieb, E., N., *Human Anatomy and Physiology.* California: Benjamin/Cummings Science Publishing.

McCormack, W., *Lost for words: Dyslexia at second-level and beyond. A practical guide for parents and teachers.* Dublin: Tower Press.

McLoughlin, D., Leather, C., and Stringer, P., *The Adult Dyslexic: Interventions and Outcomes.* London: Whurr.

Ott, Philomena., *How to Detect and Manage Dyslexia: A Reference and Resource Manual.* Oxford: Heinemann.

Reid, Gavin., *Dyslexia: A Practitioner's Handbook.* Chichester: Wiley.

Smythe, Ian., *The Dyslexia Handbook.* Reading: The British Dyslexia Association.

Temple, R., *Your Child: Dyslexia: Practical and Easy to Follow Advice.* Shaftesbury, Dorset: Element Books.

Wallace Gillet, J., and Temple, C., *Understanding Reading Problems: Assessment and Instruction.* Harper Collins.

Willows, D., Kruk, R., and Corcos, E., *Visual Processes in Reading and Reading Disabilities.* Hillsdale: Erlbaum.

199

Appendix I

Glossary of terms frequently used in educational assessments

Note: If an Educational Psychologist or other specialist has assessed your child, you will have probably received a written report. Below is a list of terms that frequently appear on such reports. Each term has a brief explanation. Remember that different professionals use various tests, but as these test are often revised, this list is by no means definitive!

Accommodations: Special allowances that are made for individuals with Specific Learning Difficulties within the classroom or during state examinations. Examples include using spellcheckers, tape recorders, and extra time for completing examinations or assignments.

Acquired dyslexia: Any symptoms usually associated with dyslexia caused by trauma or damage to the brain, such as a head injury or a brain tumour.

Agnomia: A difficulty in naming objects. The "tip of the tongue" effect.

Articulation: the ability to produce speech sounds clearly. Children with poor articulation will often distort speech sounds, resulting in mispronunciation of words, such as "Globes" for "Gloves".

Assistive technology: Any piece of equipment or system that helps kids with a learning disability by pass, work around or compensate for the specific difficulties. Examples include spellchecker, word processors and tape recorders.

Attention deficit (hyperactivity) disorder (ADD/ADHD): A severe difficulty in focusing and maintaining attention. Behaviour can include noticeable over-activity, distractibility, and/or impulsivity.

Auditory discrimination: The ability to identify the differences between speech sounds necessary for efficient language use and learning to read.

Auditory memory: The ability to remember what is heard (words, numbers and stories) in both short-term and long-term memory.

Auditory processing: The ability of individuals with normal hearing to understand spoken language.

Auditory sequencing: The ability to remember the order of items given orally in a sequential list.

Audiologist: A specialist who is trained in hearing disorders.

Attention: Selective focus on what is important while screening our distractions.

Bilateral: The ability to move both sides of the body at the same time, for example raising the right hand and the left leg simultaneously.

Brain injury: The physical damage of the tissue or structure of the brain that happens before, during or after birth. Damage caused by an accident may be referred to as Traumatic Brain Injury.

Cognitive ability: The ability to think, reason and solve problems. This is a broad range of aspects that are measured in a standard IQ test.

Congenital: A trait which exists from the time of birth.

Cross-laterality: Using opposite sides of the body for different tasks such as using the right-eye for all eye tasks but using the left-hand for all hand tasks.

Cursive: Handwriting that is joined up in a continuous flowing manner, during which a word, which is written in lower case letters, can be formed form beginning to end without lifting the pen from the page.

Diagnostic tests: Test used to measure specific ability over a range of areas such as reading comprehension, spelling, writing, etc.

Discrepancy: A marked difference between the scores achieved on two measure of ability, such as differences in Verbal and Performance Scores on the Wechsler Intelligence Scale (WISC-III)

Distractibility: The tendency for one's attention to be easily drawn from the task on hand or paying excessive attention to minor details with a lack of attention to major aspects.

Dominance profile: Established preference for side of the body used for a set task or function. It can apply to the hands, feet, eyes and ears. Also referred to as "Laterality". Individuals who have mixed dominance, for example, right-handed and left-footed, are said to have "mixed laterality".

Dyscalculia: A marked difficulty in understanding and using symbols or functions needed during arithmetic calculations.

Dysgraphia: A marked difficulty in producing handwriting that is legible at an age-appropriate speed.

Dysnomia: A marked difficulty in remembering or recalling words during oral or written language tasks.

Dyspraxia: A severe difficulty in planning and performing sensory/motor tasks. Can include difficulties maintaining balance while carrying out gross motor activities such as hopping, riding a bike, walking a straight line or difficulties with finer motor skills such as tying buttons, shoelaces or copying from the blackboard. Also know as "Developmental Co-ordination Disorder", "Clumsy Child Syndrome" "Sensory Integration Problems".

Expressive language: The ability to organise thoughts and express them verbally to convey meaning to others.

Fine motor skills: The controlled movement of the fingers and hands while performing activities such as handwriting, closing/opening buttons, threading beads onto a string.

Gross motor skills: The controlled movement of large muscles during activities such as walking, hopping and jumping.

Impulsivity: Tendency to behave without thinking about possible consequences.

Individual educational plans (IEP): A written plan which describes strategies for supporting a child in an educational environment, as a result of an assessment of their individual needs.

Kinaesthetic: The use of the sense of touch or feel. For example, using a finger to trace a letter to aid memorisation of the pattern of the letter.

Mathematical computation: The ability to manipulate numbers to add, subtract, multiply and divide correctly.

Mathematical reasoning: The ability to comprehend number, space and time relationships and concepts.

Mental age: A measure of the child's intelligence with respect to his or her chronological age.

Mnemonic: Techniques to aid recall from memory such as "Thirty days hath September …." Often used to aid recall of spelling rules.

Morphology: The study of the structure of words.

Multi-sensory learning: The combined use of all the sensory modalities during learning - hearing, sight, smell, touch, and taste.

National educational psychological service (NEPS): A dedicated agency of the Department of Education in Ireland, established in 1999, to oversee and provide the assessment of children with learning difficulties, to collaborate with parents and teachers on the individual needs of children, and to advise on policies and strategies within the field of Education.

Occupational therapist: A person who helps improve fine motor skills like cutting, holding pencils, etc.

Ophthalmologist: A medical doctor who has specialist training in the diagnosis and treatment of eye diseases and defects.

Optician: A person who is qualified to make and supply glasses and contact lenses.

Optometrist: A person who is trained to detect defects in vision and as a result to prescribe corrective lenses.

Oral language skills: The ability to understand and express spoken language. (See Receptive Language and Expressive Language)

Paediatrician: Medical doctor who is trained to work with infants, children and adolescents in the areas of growth and development including motor, sensory and behavioural development.

Perception: The ability of a person to receive, organise and integrate information from the sense organs in a meaningful way.

Phoneme: The smallest unit of sound distinguishable. The English language contains 44 phonemes.

Phonetic ability: The blending and combining of the discrete sounds to produce a word when reading or spelling. (Also known as "Phonological Awareness")

Physical therapist: A person who helps improve motor and sensory functions to increase the ability to perform daily tasks like walking, hopping, ball throwing, etc.

Pragmatics: The ability to maintain eye-contact, understand body language of others, take turns in a conversation, stick to the subject, and maintain other appropriate social conventions during social interaction. (Also known as "Social Language Skills")

Psychiatrist: Medical doctor who diagnoses and treats, severe behavioural and emotional problems. Treatment normally involves prescribing medication.

Psychologist (clinical): Provides psychological and intellectual assessment and treatment for mental and emotional health. Treatment is limited to therapy intervention.

Psychologist (educational): Provides psychological and intellectual assessment for learning difficulties and disabilities, and advises on suitable educational programmes to the needs of the individual. (See Individual Educational Plans - **IEPs**)

Receptive language: The ability to listen to, remember and understand spoken language, and to understand written language. Receptive language skills include listening and reading.

Remediation: Methods of instruction to address or correct difficulties detected in a student's learning profile.

Semantics: Understand word meanings (definitions) and relationships between words (opposites, figures of speech etc).

Sensory integration: The ability to perceive discrete stimuli and to combine them into a meaningful whole generating an appropriate response.

Sequential memory: A specific order of items to be remembered like days of the week, months of the year, letters in a word, counting, order of words in sentences, etc.

Spatial orientation: The position of an object or person in space in relation to a reference point; the accurate interpretation of the position of an object as being behind, before, above, below or to the side.

Spatial relationship: Comprehending the positions of two or more objects in relation to oneself and in relation to each other.

Speech and language therapist: A person who is trained to assess and develop intervention for children with speech and language delays.

Syntax: Understanding rules for putting words into meaningful sentences (correct grammar, position of words, etc).

Tactile discrimination: The ability to identify and match objects by touching and feeling.

Unilateral: The ability to move one side of the body without moving the other.

Visual closure: The ability to recognise or identify an object, despite the fact that part of it is missing.

Visual coordination and pursuit: The ability to follow and track objects and symbols with coordinated eye movements.

Visual discrimination: The ability to visually discriminate differences in shape, size, and formation of letters and objects.

Visual figure-ground discrimination: The ability to see objects in the foreground and background and to separate them meaningfully.

Visual memory: The ability to remember what is seen in both short-term and long-term memory tasks.

Visual-motor coordination: The ability to relate vision with body movements, such as hand-to-eye co-ordination tasks.

Visual perception: The identification, interpretation and organisation of visual data received through the eye.

Visual sequencing: The ability to remember the order of items that is presented visually.

Word-attack skills: A child's ability to decode unknown words while reading, based on application of phonic skills.

Written language skills: An assessment of the child's skills to communicate through writing, which may include handwriting skills, grammar and word usage, and written expression of thoughts and ideas.

Appendix 2

Essential words that a reader must be able to recognise and spell

One quarter of all reading material is made up of the following 12 words:

a	and	he	I
in	is	it	of
that	the	to	was

One third of all reading material is made of the following 32 words:

a	and	he	I
in	is	it	of
that	the	to	was
all	*are*	*as*	*at*
be	*but*	*for*	*had*
have	*him*	*his*	*not*
on	*one*	*said*	*so*
they	*we*	*with*	*you*

One half of all reading material is made up of the following 100 words:

a	**and**	**the**	**I**
in	**is**	**it**	**of**
that	**he**	**to**	**was**
all	*are*	*as*	*at*
be	*but*	*for*	*had*
have	*him*	*his*	*not*
on	*one*	*said*	*so*
they	*we*	*with*	*you*
about	an	back	been
before	big	by	call
came	can	come	could
did	do	down	first
from	get	go	has

her	here	if	into
just	like	little	look
made	make	me	more
much	must	my	new
no	now	off	old
only	or	other	our
out	over	right	see
she	some	their	them
then	there	this	two
up	want	well	went
were	what	when	where
which	who	will	your

The Dolch Basic Sight Vocabulary

The Dolch Basic Sight Vocabulary consists of 220 words, (100 are already present in the previous lists), which represent up to three quarters for of all words used in school books, library books, newspapers, and magazines.

and	you	let	be	into	go	drink	an
me	away	all	once	I	with	ate	three
from	that	tell	am	what	ran	must	round
then	about	ride	come	of	try	grow	us
white	run	see	under	work	seven	gave	sing
can	want	find	sleep	today	this	ten	sit
in	his	walk	four	yes	little	kind	six
live	was	two	no	do	now	pretty	clean
if	pick	is	like	down	there	their	blue
by	here	but	up	has	or	start	bring
not	don't	know	yellow	over	a	those	buy
read	on	think	could	get	fast	together	fall
made	got	how	look	who	new	did	been
ask	long	at	say	have	put	write	carry
your	said	play	thank	green	every	always	wish
the	he	red	were	right	will	pull	use
for	my	five	would	to	they	much	came
went	good	please	we	she	where	shall	just
one	small	help	big	her	take	out	upon
for	are	too	going	so	off	cut	give
stop	make	saw	had	as	it	myself	both
funny	some	jump	around	eat	old	laugh	brown
may	why	warm	first	hold	draw	only	eight
many	never	when	does	own	because	light	fly
keep	any	them	very	done	which	goes	open
not	after	before	wash	call	best	our	him
these	full	better	soon	its	black	again	show
cold	hurt						

Index